David
Robinson

David Robinson

by Bill Gutman

Rainbow Bridge ®
Troll Associates

Introduction

He's known as the Admiral . . . with good reason. He's called a superstar . . . with good reason. He's rated as one of the best centers in the National Basketball Association . . . with good reason. And he's earned the reputation as one of the good guys in sports . . . with good reason.

In fact, there isn't much that David Robinson doesn't do without a good reason. The 7'1", 235-pound center of the San Antonio Spurs is not only one of the best, but one of the brightest players in the game. He's also a player who didn't take the usual route to basketball stardom. If you asked David Robinson back in the early 1980s if he thought he would be banging elbows with the best the NBA had to offer, he probably would have laughed.

That's because David didn't plan to be a professional athlete. He planned to be a career officer in the United States Navy. He planned it very carefully and for a long time. Everything he did was geared to that end. And he was well on the way to making it happen when he was appointed to the Naval Academy in 1983.

But then something unexpected occurred. While he was at the Naval Academy David Robinson grew, and grew, and then grew some more. During that time, he also began to look at basketball as more than the enjoyable recreational activity it had always been to him. It became more of a passion, another way for him to express himself creatively.

It was only then that David began to look at the game the way all great players have. The difference was that most of them start early, living on playgrounds with bent rims, playing game after game in hot, sweaty gyms, looking for teams to join and coaches to learn from. They eat, drink, and sleep basketball. It becomes their life.

David Robinson did it his way. He didn't take hold of the game; it took hold of him. Now it's David who won't let go. He's been an all-star, the NBA Defensive Player of the Year, and the league's scoring champion. He's mentioned in the same breath as Hakeem Olajuwon, Shaquille O'Neal, and Patrick Ewing.

He's one of the best.

David Robinson

Chapter 1
Navy Brat

David Robinson grew up surrounded by the United States Navy. The reason was simple. His father, Ambrose Robinson, was a career navy man, a sonar technician assigned to the huge naval base at Norfolk, Virginia. David was actually born in Key West, Florida, on August 6, 1965. But when he was very young the family moved to Virginia Beach, Virginia, because his father was assigned to the Norfolk base.

Ambrose Robinson was originally from Little Rock, Arkansas, while David's mother, Freda, came from Columbia, South Carolina. But all roads eventually led to Virginia, where David, his younger sister, Kim, and brother, Chuck, spent most of their childhood.

Being a "navy brat" wasn't always easy. David's father was often at sea for months at a time, away from his family. David's mother worked, too. Freda Robinson was a nurse whose hours were always changing. That meant that once they were old enough, the three children were often left alone. Not having their parents around wasn't easy, but it turned into a positive experience.

"We always knew the difference between right and wrong," David explained. "We had a lot of responsibilities, but we had freedom, too. For that reason, I never felt any desire to break loose."

Their responsibilities included cooking, cleaning, gardening, and, of course, getting their homework done. The Robinsons always left detailed instructions for their children telling them exactly what had to be done. Education was always very important, so homework was a priority. All three children had their chores and almost always got them done on time. They rarely even thought about not doing them.

Discipline became a big part of David's life early on. That's not unusual for children of military service personnel. Some kids rebel against it. David, on the other hand, seemed to welcome it. He liked a set routine, knowing just what he had to do and when he had to do it. He would apply the lessons of discipline to nearly everything he did when he grew up.

There is little doubt that Ambrose Robinson was the most important influence in his son's life. David always missed his father when the elder Robinson was away at sea. When he returned home, Mr. Robinson made his family the number one priority. They would always do things together, whether it be going on vacation or just finding a fun recreational activity. The Robinsons enjoyed bowling, fishing, and other sports. These were happy times, and the children looked forward to their father's return.

Ambrose Robinson also liked doing jobs himself. He would often build and repair things around the house, and young David was always at his heels. He watched his father carefully and tried to copy the things he did.

When David was 12, his father brought home a big television as a present for his wife. Before he could finish setting it up, however, Mr. Robinson had to ship out once again. Young David took right over and assembled the rest of the television himself. He was really proud of doing that, but he always gave credit to his father.

"My Dad was everything," David said, in later years. "He was the person I patterned myself after. I never had any sports role models as a youngster."

Another reason for that could have been that sports really didn't play a big part in young David's life. It was really education and learning that occupied his time. When he was in the first grade he was already enrolled in a program for gifted children. That was just the beginning.

His mother also remembers his math wizardry in the grocery store. He would walk alongside her as she put various items in the cart. By the time they reached the register David always knew just how much the cost would be. He did the addition in his head without a pencil and paper or a calculator.

As he got older, he developed many interests.

By the time he was 14 he was already taking advanced computer courses. He seemed to enjoy subjects that had exact answers, like science and math, rather than those that relied on interpretation, such as English.

He also loved music from an early age. When he wanted to learn an instrument, he would begin teaching it to himself. In his early teenage years, he taught himself to play the piano and French horn, an unusual combination. Later, he would become quite good on the saxophone.

Sports in those days was something he put on the back burner. Sure he played some baseball, football, and basketball with his friends, but it was simply for fun, nothing more. David admits he had no real passion for any of those sports and didn't pursue them on an organized level. He didn't see athletics as a means of expression. In fact, his first experience with school sports was not a good one.

It happened when he was a freshman at Green Run High School in Virginia Beach. He started there in the fall of 1979 when he was 14. Though his father stood 6'6" tall, David grew slowly in his early years. For awhile, in fact, his family didn't think he would even be as tall as his father. But in his early teens he had a growth spurt, and by the time he reached Green Run he was more than six feet tall. As a result he decided to go out for basketball.

Up till then he hadn't really played a lot of ball. He certainly wasn't one of those kids who hung around the playground all day looking for a game and staying until it was dark. His experience with the finer points of basketball was limited. So it wasn't surprising that he didn't stay with the team long.

David never talked much about what happened. There was a story that he left the team after he was benched. But it's more likely that he quit simply because he saw there were better players and thought he would be cut anyway. Apparently, he just didn't have the motivation to stay. So his focus returned to the classroom and his studies.

By his sophomore year he was 6'4". Yet he didn't even think about going out for the team again. In fact, he wouldn't play any more basketball at Green Run. Had he stayed there all four of his high school years, he might never have played basketball again. But all that would change in 1982 when Ambrose Robinson decided to retire from the navy after 20 years of service.

When Mr. Robinson took a civilian job in the northern part of the state, the family packed up and moved to Manassas, Virginia, which was in the Washington, D.C., area. David would have to transfer to Osbourn Park High School and would be starting a new life in more ways than one.

Looking back on his childhood in later years, David knows he had something special, although it took a little more life experience to make him realize it.

"When I was younger, it never dawned on me what a good life I was leading," he said. "Now I see friends who don't talk to their parents, their brothers, their sisters, and I think how sad it is that they're missing out on all that love."

Chapter 2
New Directions

By the time David reached Osbourn Park High in November 1982, he was nearly 6'7" tall. Because he had transferred after the school year started, everybody quickly heard about the new kid and checked him out. One of those who heard about him was basketball coach Art Payne. Like any basketball coach, Payne was naturally curious about the 6'7" kid who had just entered his school.

"I wasn't real excited at first," Payne recalls, "because you sometimes get these tall kids who just aren't interested in playing. We already had one kid who was about that tall on the team, but we didn't have a history of having real big kids at the school back then."

So Coach Payne approached David and asked him if he was interested in playing basketball. David said yes, but in a kind of halfhearted way. Then something else began to happen that may have decided it for him.

"All day long kids kept going up to him and saying, 'Hey, you've got to play basketball, you've got to play basketball,'" Art Payne remembered. "By the end of the day he had been inundated by students telling him he had to play basketball. It was almost as if he had no way out because the kids were so enthusiastic about him playing. He just couldn't say no."

David didn't practice that first day because he hadn't had the required physical exam. But after that, he never missed a practice or a game. Art Payne remembers him as being very coachable, "just a super kid to work with."

But this isn't one of those stories where the new kid comes out for the team and becomes an instant star and the school hero. David had a long way to go on the basketball court, and what's more, he knew it.

"I didn't play a whole lot of street ball," he said, "so I didn't have the moves, the intuitive things that a lot of kids learned over the years on the playgrounds. At Osbourn High basketball was more work than fun. I always knew I could prove myself academically. But with basketball then, it was just a matter of trying to stick it out."

Though he decided to stick it out this time, David never neglected his academic work. He had already decided that his goal was to secure an appointment to the United States Naval Academy. He liked the idea of the structure offered by the academy, and also the security of a career in the navy. He was also impressed by the math and engineering programs offered at the academy, and that was the most important thing in his life then.

Perhaps, however, it was an old-fashioned dose of fate that forced him to concentrate more on basketball, more than he might have even planned. Osbourn Park had another 6'7" kid who was penciled in as the starting center that year. But a short time after David arrived, the other kid suffered a bad ankle sprain and couldn't play. Before he knew it, David Robinson was the starting center on a basketball team that played in a very tough league.

Art Payne had been around long enough to know that David was what is called a "project," a player who has potential, but one who couldn't be expected to blossom into an instant star.

"I didn't know David that well and as a consequence didn't push real hard with him," the coach said. "He had an awful lot to learn but you could already see that if he stuck with it, he was going to be a quality player."

The coach described David as tall and somewhat gangly that year, with very good agility for a kid who was still growing. His movements on the court were very smooth and he had soft hands, which enabled him to catch even tough passes. It was simply a matter of learning the finer points of the game, practicing them through repetition, and then putting them into practice. In basketball, as in other sports, that doesn't happen overnight.

David also didn't realize back then what the role of a dominant player could be. Coach Payne feels that, too, might have held him back somewhat. His size and agility enabled him to be a good rebounder, but he still didn't have a really good shooting touch.

Because his instincts for the game were still not fully developed, David made mistakes that year that he wouldn't repeat later. He still didn't react automatically to certain situations. Just a moment's hesitation, and a play could be botched. Whenever that happened, David was smart enough to realize it right away.

Coach Payne recalls a game in the district playoffs when the final seconds would determine who won. "The plan was to loop a pass to David under the basket," the coach said. "The ball was right on target, but instead of catching it, then going up for the hoop, David tried to tip the ball in. He missed. The other team got the rebound and wound up with a basket and free throw. That was the game.

"But before I could even say anything to him, David came out and said, 'Coach, I should have grabbed the ball and gone right up with it.' It was just a matter of his instincts catching up with his good mind."

With David in the middle, Osbourn Park put together a .500 season. Despite his inexperience, David emerged as the team's leading scorer and rebounder. He averaged about 14 points a game, but was inconsistent. There were nights when he had more than 20, and other nights when he was in single figures. Had he played more and developed his instincts, Coach Payne said the team could have been special.

"We were a hair away from being a real solid team," the coach explained, "with the difference being David's inexperience. Had he played more before coming here our record could have easily been something like 18-6 or even 20-4. It was his inconsistency that hurt us.

"Also, he still hadn't developed that real enthusiasm for the game that the great players have. I could sense it was starting to come toward the end of the season. That's when he began to sense what he was capable of really doing out there."

As an example, Coach Payne recalled one game in which two starters were suspended for disciplinary reasons. The team played terribly in the first half and was trailing badly when they went into the locker room for intermission. It was one of the few times Coach Payne lost it.

"I came in and threw the clipboard down, really hot, then put my coaching face on and began chewing them out. David was sitting in front of me, kind of moped over. But when I started screaming he came to attention, just sat up like a board, like he was already in the military. It really tickled me. But the funny thing was that in the second half he was really fired up and we darn near won the ballgame."

David quickly became a popular presence at Osbourn Park High. Coach Payne describes him as a "people person" who loved being around his friends and talking with them.

"David always talked about a lot of things," the coach said. "Sometimes I would give him a ride home after practice and our conversations were really interesting. He had a real wide spectrum of things he liked to talk about."

Even though David wound up being named to the All-Area and All-District teams, as well as being voted Osbourn's Most Valuable Player, basketball was still far from his number one priority. Coach Payne said that he felt David would have been just as satisfied to be a concert pianist as a basketball player then. David still didn't have any basketball idols and his only goal was the Naval Academy.

Like many high school seniors around the country, David took the college board exam and waited anxiously for his score. When he learned he had scored an impressive 1320 (out of a perfect 1400), he was overjoyed. That number was more important to him that any number of points he might have scored in a basketball game. In fact, basketball still didn't figure in his Naval Academy plans.

"I didn't care whether I played basketball at the academy or not," David admitted. "I just wanted to get good grades and fit in."

Top high school basketball players have to go through college recruiting. The top players are usually deluged by college coaches and recruiters trying to convince them to come to their school. Most NBA stars remember going through that hectic and exciting period. David didn't. Many schools just weren't interested.

Art Payne remembers one of their games when Terry Holland, the head coach of the University of Virginia, was in the crowd. Holland was looking at a kid on the opposing team. David played his usual game and Holland showed absolutely no interest in him. Coaches at that level don't want a "project." They want stars.

There was one thing that worried David right up until the moment when his appointment to the academy arrived. That was his height. The height limit for midshipmen entering the academy was 6'6". That could have finished David right there, except for one exemption. It allowed 5 percent of the incoming class to be as tall as 6'8". David was still growing, but was just a shade over 6'7" when the appointment came. He had made it by less than one inch.

Fortunately for David, once midshipmen enter the academy they are allowed to remain even if they continue to grow—and David Robinson still had quite a bit of growing to do. He graduated from Osbourn Park High in the spring of 1983 and prepared to enter the United States Naval Academy at Annapolis, Maryland.

Art Payne has never forgotten the tall, lanky youngster who played just one year of ball for him. David made quite an impression in the time he was at Osbourn Park.

"Even if David had never been a basketball player he was still a super person," Art Payne said, "the type of kid that any parent would like to say, 'That's my son.' He spoke well, dressed well, and was well-mannered. David wasn't the type to party it up. He was simply a real all-American kid. I don't know how else to say it."

Chapter 3
Navy—
The Early Years

David Robinson was appointed to the Naval Academy on the basis of his academic achievements and the kind of all-around person he had become. But that didn't mean that the people at the academy hadn't noticed his size and the fact that he was on his high school basketball team. All service academies have active sports programs and recruit athletes.

That's why assistant basketball coach Pete Hermann paid a visit to David's home to talk about the basketball program.

"I started by asking David why he wanted to go to the academy," Hermann related. "His answer was that he felt Navy was one of the finest schools in the country for math, which was going to be his major. He also said he felt that he could be successful in life if he graduated from the academy. Those were his prime goals, and basketball wasn't a part of it."

That didn't stop Hermann and head coach Paul Evans from taking a look at David the player. They, too, could see that he lacked experience, but his natural physical tools told them something else.

"We felt he could become a solid running foward," said Pete Hermann. "His hands were pretty good and he could run. What he needed then was more strength and stamina, but we felt that was something he could develop. What none of us envisioned those first times we saw him was that he would eventually become a center."

David entered the Naval Academy in the late summer of 1983. Though just 18, he was confident that he could handle both the academic program and the naval training. He always preferred a disciplined existence, and he would certainly have that at Annapolis. What made David go out for the basketball team as a freshman isn't quite clear. Maybe he felt that playing would be a good diversion from the intensity of his studies and training.

He certainly didn't approach the sport with real enthusiasm. He would later admit to sitting in math class and saying to himself, "Oh, brother, I have to go to basketball practice today."

Once he approached a teammate who was always shooting and practicing, and working on his game, and asked him why he never got tired of all that practice. Even the coaches noticed his less-than-great attitude.

"It was apparent that basketball wasn't real important to him then," Coach Hermann said. "I can barely remember him in practice that year. There just wasn't much he liked about playing then. It was really a struggle for him all year."

The Navy Midshipmen might not have been a top ten team, but they still played Division I basketball. (Division I teams are from the country's largest schools and often have tough, top-rated teams.) For a kid with just a single year of high school ball under his belt, it wasn't an easy transition.

For one thing, he was still growing. He was now 6'9". Because he was growing so quickly, he was somewhat awkward his freshman year as he continued to develop both physically and mentally.

Point guard Doug Wojcik entered the academy the same time as David and saw what it was like for his new friend that first year. "I just don't think David had a real awareness of his ability his freshman year," Wojcik said. "We had a starting center named Cliff Maurer that year. Cliff was about 6'11" and just an average player. But David watched him closely all year and learned a lot by playing behind him. Yet there really was still no way to tell how good he was going to be."

So David spent his freshman year learning the game and also learning how to budget and balance his time. At the service academies there isn't much idle time to hang out or party. There is a lot the cadets have to learn and athletes have more business to attend to than others.

"You've got to be able to balance the academics and the basketball," David said. "It's a pretty good mix, though, because if you work hard at both you aren't going to get too caught up in one or the other. So budgeting your time isn't something you think a whole lot about. You really don't have much of a choice."

During his freshman year, David managed to budget his time well. He earned a 3.22 grade-point average (out of a possible 4.0), but it wasn't easy. He realized it took something of an adjustment to function at a service academy, but there were also rewards to life at the academy.

"Homework varies from too much to way too much," he said. "In fact, at first everything seemed unfair. There was no radio or TV in the hall and no McDonald's. But there is responsibility and respect. Those are the things that keep you going. You learn to cope instead of complain. Besides, I like the guys here. We wear uniforms and march, but we also find some time to party."

Whatever partying he did, David also had to work hard in the classroom and on the basketball court. An athlete has to be in great shape to play ball at Navy. Service academy basketball teams generally aren't the tallest around, so they make up for it with scrap and hustle, and with very sound fundamentals. They usually play a very unselfish, team-oriented game if they want to succeed.

Navy did that well in 1983-84. There were some talented players and a core of seniors for leadership. The club went 24-8, the most victories in Navy history. Sophomore forward Vernon Butler led the team in scoring with a 14.7 average and in rebounding with an 8.7 per game mark. Another good sophomore was Kylor Whitaker, a shooting guard who scored at a ten-point clip.

As for David, he played in 28 games, averaging 7.6 points and 4.0 rebounds per contest. Very modest numbers. He also blocked 37 shots. Again, that wasn't very impressive considering his size, quickness, and agility. But then again, he only played about 13 minutes a game. One of the bright spots was his 62.3 shooting percentage. That was the best mark on the team, though the lefty center took the majority of his shots from close in. His best games of the year were a 19-point effort against Campbell College and an 11-rebound performance against William and Mary.

When the season ended, David joined an intramural boxing program in order to stay active. That resulted in a slight break in one of the bones in his hand. When the doctor examined the injury, he told the coaches something that surprised them.

"There's still a lot of growth left in this youngster," the doctor said.

David spent the summer of 1984 doing things that indicated that basketball was perhaps becoming more important to him. He worked with weights, adding strength and size. In addition, he played street ball in an Urban Coalition League in Washington, D.C. There's no better way to learn the little tricks of the game than to play in a street league in a large city. That can be a basketball education in itself.

When David returned to the academy in the fall the coaches took one look at him and realized the doctor was right. He had grown another two inches and had gained 20 pounds. He was now a full 6'11" tall and weighed 215 pounds. There was also no doubt what position he had to play. David was now a full-fledged center.

When basketball season rolled around, the coaches decided that they had to make some adjustments. Cliff Maurer had graduated and David was now the only true center on the team. He would have to be the starter and he would have to come through. The coaches made no bones about that.

"Coach Evans came right out and told David that if he was good this year, the team would be pretty good, but if he wasn't good, the team wasn't going to be good," said Pete Hermann. "I'm sure that put some pressure on him. We also decided to center the offense around him. The other guys on the team saw that if we got the ball in to David we were going to score points and win games."

Because David still wasn't an experienced center they kept it simple. Instead of moving around in the pivot, David always set up in the same spot on the left side and the other players worked to get the ball in to him. There wasn't a whole lot of movement or cutting. David was simply down close to the hoop and told to look for quick, turnaround jump shots.

"We basically wanted him to catch the ball and score," said Pete Hermann. "That's what he did at first. Then, as he got more experience and saw he could score, he began to expand his game, driving to the basket more, faking and throwing the hook shot. But during his sophomore year it stayed pretty basic."

The team won its first three games that year, with David tossing in a career high 29 points in the third game against American University. After the club lost to Penn State they traveled to Illinois to participate in the four-team Saluki Shootout Tournament. It would prove to be a turning point. In the first game, Navy had to meet the host club, Southern Illinois.

Southern Illinois had a fine team and just seemed a bit better than the Navy Midshipmen. But David had an outstanding night, and Navy kept it close. The Southern Illinois Salukis ended up winning, 75-72, but David wound up with a 31-point night. He was really beginning to make his presence felt.

Navy then went up against Western Illinois in the consolation game and David was even better. He was hitting his turnaround jumper all night, going inside for slams and rebounding at both ends of the floor. When it ended, Navy had an 80-74 victory and David had career bests of 37 points and 18 rebounds. That wasn't all. He was also named the Most Valuable Player in the tournament, a rare honor for a player whose team finished in third place.

"I think those two games in the Saluki Shootout were a turning point for David," said teammate Doug Wojcik. "We continually went down to him in both games and he responded. From that point on he realized he could be a pretty good player. Of course, he turned out to be much more than that."

From there, the "Middies" rolled to ten straight

wins, with David continuing as the focal point of the attack. The other starters—Butler, Whitaker, Wojcik and Cliff Rees—were all solid players. There wasn't much depth, but the starting five were a very good basketball team, especially with the big man in the middle becoming a real star.

There was one game in the streak against Lafayette that really tested David. The Lafayette defense was doing a great job to keep him from getting the ball, fronting him and cutting off the passing lanes. At one point late in the first half David was getting discouraged and beginning to lose his aggressiveness. Coach Evans even sat him down on the bench for a few minutes.

The game would eventually go into double overtime, and it was David who got most of the key Navy baskets toward the end of regulation and then in OT. The Middies finally won, 74-71, as David contributed 27 points, six rebounds, and seven big blocks. He called it a "fair performance," but his teammates saw again just how key he had become to their team and their season.

"We know now we can only go as far as David goes," said Vernon Butler.

In the tenth victory of the streak, David set yet another career high of 39 points as Navy topped East Carolina University, 87-68. His success and that of the team was slowly making the court game more popular at the academy. Fans jammed into Halsey Field House to see the Middies play. There was a time when empty seats were the order of the day. Now, the 5,000-seat field house was standing room only.

The Middies would lose just three more games during the regular season as David continued to excel. But he still wasn't completely there. Coach Hermann said one weakness David had was a tendency to run out of gas late in some games.

"It was a matter of conditioning," the coach said. "It wasn't that David didn't work hard. By that time, he did. I think it was just that he wasn't yet completely developed physically. But we knew that would come in time."

Coach Evans, who worked David hard in practice and could be critical of his play at times, also saw the talent and unlimited potential in his big center.

"There aren't many 6'11" centers who have his hands, his shooting touch, and his ability to run the floor," Evans said. "David can block a shot at one end and dunk at the other. He's still learning to be aggressive and to go to his right. But we're slowly allowing him to do more things."

The 1984-85 Midshipmen turned out to be the best Navy squad in history. They finished the year at 26-6 and began to show that they could compete with anyone. The biggest moment probably came when the team received its first bid to the NCAA (National Collegiate Athletic Association) tournament in 25 years. Navy teams aren't supposed to be that good.

Not wanting to look bad, the Middies went out and upset powerful Louisiana State before finally losing to Maryland, a team that made sure it double- and triple-teamed David for nearly the entire game.

Ken Denlinger, a sportswriter for *The Washington Post*, felt the Maryland team knew that unless David was checked he could beat them.

"For most of the game today," Denlinger wrote, "Navy's center found himself with a Maryland player to his immediate left, a Maryland player to his immediate right and a Maryland player hand-checking him from behind. It was the first time Goliath ever got frightened by David."

Navy led early in the Maryland game, but the Terps' relentless pressure eventually wore David and his teammates down. Pete Hermann remembers it as one of those games in which David ran out of gas.

"We really emphasized to him the need for conditioning and told him we hoped he'd work hard at it during the off-season and the summer," Coach Hermann said.

David ended his sophomore year averaging a team-leading 23.6 points a game, a far cry from his modest 7.6 average as a freshman. He also led the club with 370 rebounds for an 11.6 per game average. He had 128 blocked shots and a field goal percentage of 64.4 percent. He was ECAC (East Coast Athletic Conference) South Player of the Year and first team All-East. He was second among Division I sophomores in scoring, and led them all in rebounding, field goal percentage, and blocked shots.

He wasn't yet a bona-fide All-American, but he was getting closer. And by this time, David Robinson was beginning to want it.

Chapter 4

A Decision for the Future

The tremendous improvement in David's game his sophomore year was a reason for cheer around the Naval Academy. He still had two more years remaining and there were thoughts of the team reaching even greater heights. But for David, there was a new kind of pressure. And it didn't have to do with shooting and rebounding. At least, not in a direct sense.

Any time a 6'11" center begins showing outstanding skills and dominating his peers, another whole group of people begin looking at him. They are the coaches, scouts, and other players in the National Basketball Association. The pros. Even the college coaches were talking about it. Ed Tapscott, the coach at American University, wasn't alone when he spoke about David.

"He's already one of the top big men in the East, no doubt about it," said Tapscott. "He's a terrific athlete, runs the court like a deer, and he's got great hands. He gets better every time out. He's definitely got pro potential."

There was one kicker. Any graduate of a service academy, including athletes, is bound to do at least five years of active duty in that particular branch of the service. Very few athletes have returned after five years away and made it as a professional athlete. One notable exception was Roger Staubach, who was an All-American quarterback at Navy in the 1960s. Staubach served five years of duty, then returned to the Dallas Cowboys, eventually becoming an All-Pro and later a Hall of Famer.

But there was an out for service academy athletes who began to think about pro ball. If an athlete thought he might not want to fulfill his five-year obligation and try to play pro ball, he had to transfer out of the academy after his sophomore year. He could then complete his education and athletic eligibility at a regular four-year university. But if he stayed at the academy beyond his sophomore year, he was locked into the five-year obligation.

There's no doubt that David hadn't even thought about this remotely before his sophomore year. As a freshman, he was just another backup center who attracted absolutely no attention. But as a sophomore, his improvement was incredible. Suddenly, he was becoming a major force. And in basketball, a 6'11" major force can't hide.

So it wasn't surprising that speculation regarding David's future plans began. Would he leave the academy? Was he thinking about pro ball? Coach Evans felt that David would stay, as much for the academics as for basketball.

"He really wants his degree," the coach said.

Assistant coach Pete Hermann knew David even better. It was his feeling that the NBA was definitely now on David's mind. "I'm sure he thought about it from his sophomore year on, but he never talked about it much," Coach Hermann said. "Even when the idea became stronger, he still felt first and foremost that graduating from the academy would guarantee him a route to success."

Finally someone asked David. The question was asked before the academic year ended, when there was still time for David to transfer. He seemed to leave the door open, if ever so slightly.

"I don't think I'll transfer," he said, "but I'm not certain. I'll have to think about transferring because I might be missing a great opportunity to play pro ball and make a lot of money. Still, I don't see myself as a Patrick Ewing and if I spent all my time playing basketball, I might not enjoy it."

Then David continued. "I feel comfortable at the academy. When you graduate, you get a good job and a pension after 20 years."

It was almost beginning to sound as if David was fighting a battle within himself. He was still a young man with many diverse interests. There was little doubt that he enjoyed the atmosphere of the Naval Academy immensely. He was still a curious student, someone who wanted to learn. It was hard to think that he would give all that up for basketball.

"We didn't push him toward the academy," his father said, when someone asked the family about David's future. "The biggest advantage is its academic structure and togetherness. But it's his decision. I hope he stays. He feels at home there."

David had to be well aware of what he would be giving up by leaving the academy. Sure, he could make a ton of money if he became a pro star. But, as with any sport, all it takes is one injury, one wrong step that could blow out a knee, one bulging disk in the back, and a basketball career can be short-circuited or ended. If that happened, he could never get back what he lost by transferring.

David's teammate and friend, Doug Wojcik, said that a number of colleges had already been making inquiries and sending out feelers to see if David might be interested in transferring.

"The people at these schools knew that David was a quality person as well as a talented one," Wojcik said. "There was also a great deal of media pressure. The attention made David realize he had become pretty much of a household name and also that he was becoming a pretty good player. So I definitely have to believe the pros were on his mind by then."

It's really amazing how much attention David was getting because of basketball. After all, he had only been playing organized ball for three years and had been a star for just one. Yet he was already being talked about as a future star center in the NBA. Even the Naval Academy brass was aware of the possibility of losing David. But Rear Admiral

Charles R. Larsen, the academy superintendent, spoke of David in terms of a complete person, not just a basketball player. "David Robinson is the kind of kid the Naval Academy would go after if he couldn't play basketball at all," said the superintendent. "He's an excellent student and a natural leader. Those are the qualities we look for here."

Although leaving the academy was a possibility and quite a few people talked about it, it didn't become a prolonged drama. The question of will he or won't he didn't linger very far past the basketball season. It's hard to know the exact reason for David's final decision. Some felt it was simply because he hadn't played that much basketball and still couldn't envision himself an NBA star. Others pointed out that he had wanted to attend the Naval Academy for years.

David finally put it this way. "Right now I don't see any reason to leave Navy. Maybe I just don't think I'm as good as other people seem to think I am. But I like the academy. It's a tough place, but I'm happy here."

That was the end of the story for then. Some felt it was also the end of David as a pro prospect, that he would settle in for a naval career after graduation. But only time would tell. What he had done was tell everyone that he was committed to the navy, and that included at least a five-year obligation after he graduated.

When he returned for his junior year of 1985-86 David was officially listed as 6'11", 230 pounds. But it was apparent to those around him that he was very close to seven-feet, and might even hit that mark before the season ended. At any rate, he still hadn't stopped growing.

He had continued to play during the summer as a member of the United States team that played at the world championships in Barcelona, Spain. When practice back at Navy started, he looked like a stronger, more confident player. The other four starters from the previous season were also back, as were a number of the top subs. Suddenly, there was great anticipation around the entire academy. For the first time in academy history, Navy would have a basketball team to be reckoned with.

The coaches quickly formulated a game plan that would get the most out of David and his supporting cast. Again, it was a basically simple formula built around David on both offense and defense.

"David is left-handed and so am I," explained Doug Wojcik, "so we always had the offense geared toward the left side of the floor. For the most part, we went to him or looked to him every time down the floor. David just sat in the low post on the left side.

"The better teams could adjust to this and therefore had a good chance to beat us. But teams in our conference couldn't do a whole lot about it. Both Vernon Butler and Kylor Whitaker were good shooters, so they had to be guarded. They were usually able to open things up and then we could get David right back into the flow."

On defense, it was set up so the 6'8", 240-pound Butler would play the middle of the zone. That left David with more opportunities to rebound and block shots. And he did that as well as any college player in the country.

It was apparent from the opening game of the season that Navy wouldn't buckle under pressure. This was a team that could stick with just about anyone. A big test came right away when the Midshipmen traveled to Madison Square Garden in New York City to participate in the Joe Lapchick Tournament. Powerful St. John's was the host team. Led by their All-American forward, Walter Berry, the St. John's Red Storm met Navy in the opener.

The Red Storm had a fine all-around team and won the game, 66-58, but not before David and his teammates made them work for it. In fact, David was the best player on the floor, popping for 27 points and grabbing 18 rebounds. His quickness and overall defensive ability made a big impression on the knowledgeable New York fans, who gave him a huge ovation near the end of the game.

Led by David, the Middies then went on a run, winning 14 of their next 16 games. Their only losses in that period were to top-ranked national powers Syracuse and Georgia Tech. But they also beat an outstanding team when they topped DePaul, 67-64. Butler led the team with 23 points against the Blue Demons, while David corralled 16 rebounds. He didn't have to be the leading scorer for the team to win.

While he was scoring very well, his rebounding

and shot-blocking were also getting a great deal of attention. He was right up among the leaders in rebounds, while he easily led everyone in blocks. In a game against North Carolina-Wilmington in early January, David was all over the court, going after everything. When it ended, Navy had won easily and David had blocked an amazing 14 shots.

A shot-blocker like David can disrupt an offense in several ways. He may actually block five or ten shots, but how many other shots are off the mark because the shooter is aware of David's awesome presence in the middle? Players driving the lane often change the angle or trajectory of their shot, hoping the shot-blocker doesn't get it. Others are even hesitant to shoot, and look to pass the ball back out.

David continued to show amazing quickness and agility for a man his size. His stamina was improved and he could run the court as well as most smaller men. In a word, he was rapidly becoming the complete package and taking his team along with him. After winning 14 of 16 games, the Middies began to appear in the national rankings of the top 20 teams. That's a lofty position seldom attained by service academy teams.

There was no way the smaller schools could keep up with Navy. Among those, only Richmond managed to upset the Midshipmen during the season. In fact, it was Richmond that ended the 14-victory run. But after that defeat, Navy would win its next 16 straight before tasting defeat again.

In the meantime, David kept putting up

tremendous numbers. He surpassed the 30-point mark on numerous occasions, with a high of 37 against Delaware. Against another small school, Fairfield University, he scrubbed the boards to the tune of 25 rebounds. That kind of small school competition was just no match for him.

When the regular schedule ended, Navy had a 24-4 mark and now geared up for the start of tournament play. First they took their conference tourney with wins over James Madison, University of North Carolina-Wilmington, and George Mason. David had 80 points and 47 rebounds in those three games.

Now the Middies would be going to the NCAA tournament. It was time to play with the big boys again and Navy's best chance to show the country just how good it really was. Their first test would come against a very good Tulsa team. With the Middies still going to David almost every time, they beat up on Tulsa pretty badly.

The final score was 87-68, with David getting 30 points and 12 rebounds. The Middies' simple offense continued to work well. Once he had the ball, David would look for a quick turnaround jumper or the opportunity to drive. If he was double-teamed, he'd look to kick it out to an open teammate. If his teammate didn't have a shot they would reset and run the offense again.

After beating Tulsa, it looked as if Navy faced a seemingly insurmountable task. Waiting in the next round was Syracuse, a team that had beaten the Middies by 22 points early in the season. The

Syracuse Orangemen were led by guard "Pearl" Washington and center Rony Seikaly. Navy was given little chance of beating them, especially in tough tournament play.

But early on it became obvious that this wouldn't be a replay of the early season game. David was playing an especially strong game, showing his quickness and deft shooting touch, while outplaying his counterpart Seikaly. Navy had a small lead early in the second half when there was a series of bang-bang plays that might have been the turning point in the game.

Navy had the ball and went to David, as usual. With just a small opening, he made a lightning-fast move on Seikaly and scored from in close. However, he didn't do what a lot of today's players do, celebrate the hoop or look to high-five a teammate. David immediately looked for the ball and found it in the hands of Pearl Washington.

The speedy Syracuse guard was fast-breaking, taking the ball right down the center of the court. He was ahead of the field, going in for an apparent easy layup. Suddenly there was David, his long legs churning downcourt in pursuit of Washington. Just as the Pearl released the ball, David leaped into the air and blocked the shot from behind. His momentum carried him over the end line into the courtside crowd.

Meanwhile, there was a scramble for the rebound, with the ball finally being grabbed by Wendell Alexis of Syracuse. Alexis went right up into the air to lay the ball in on a put-back. Out of nowhere came big number 50 once again. David soared high to make his second clean block of what appeared to be a sure hoop. This time a Navy teammate grabbed the ball and the Middies broke downcourt, going in for a quick hoop of their own.

After that, Navy seemed to get stronger and they pulled away for a surprising 97-85 upset victory. David had played an incredible game, scoring 35 points, grabbing 11 rebounds, and blocking a number of Syracuse shots. Fouling him often didn't even help. That day he went to the line 27 times and sank 21 of them.

"Whenever I think back about David and our team during those years I always think of that sequence against Syracuse," said Doug Wojcik. "It really showed what David was all about. The entire series of plays with the two blocks was just so impressive."

The victory over Syracuse proved once and for all that this Navy team could play with anyone. But their big victory almost backfired when they unexpectedly let down their guard in their next game against little Cleveland State. They just managed to squeak by, 71-70.

Now the club was on the brink of something great. They had already gone further than any previous Navy team in an NCAA tournament. One more win in the East Regional final and the Middies would advance to the fabled Final Four.

This time Navy would be facing another outstanding team, the Duke Blue Devils. With David at the top of his game, many felt Navy had a chance to win and to go after the national championship. But it wasn't to be. Duke just had too much overall team speed for the Middies. Led by All-American guard Johnny Dawkins, Duke won easily, 71-50, ending Navy's NCAA dream. David had 23 points and 10 rebounds against the Blue Devils. But it just wasn't enough.

One person who had followed the entire Navy season with interest was Art Payne, David's high school coach at Osbourn Park. Payne had a very interesting observation about the 1985-86 Middies.

"I really thought that the Navy ball club that year was just a hair away from being the best team in the country," he said. "They had David and some other fine players. In fact, the entire starting five was strong. With a couple of more good players coming off the bench they really could have cracked the top four."

As it was, they came very close. The team set a school record by finishing at 30-5. David's outstanding numbers were just another testimonial to his performance all year. He wound up averaging 22.7 points a game on 60.7 percent shooting from the field. He also led the nation with 455 rebounds, a 13.0 average, and in blocked shots, with 207.

There was something even more incredible about that last number. As an individual, David had more blocked shots than every entire team in the country, with the exception of national champ Louisville. The Louisville Cardinals, as a team, had 213 blocks. David averaged 5.9 blocks a game all by himself.

Most major All-American polls put him on the second team, though some first team selections didn't have a true center among those chosen. There were several organizations that did put him on their first team. But there probably wasn't a college coach in the land who wouldn't want David Robinson as his starting center.

Because he had completed his junior year at the academy, there was no more talk about him leaving. But there was still speculation about his basketball future. Very few people doubted that David now had the ability to compete and probably excel in the NBA. They wondered if he might be allowed to play part-time. Or if he did serve five years, could he then return to the game?

David himself had said late in the season that he wasn't solely motivated by money.

"I don't live for money," was the way he put it. "So many people think they are automatically happy if they have it. I don't necessarily think so. It is a factor in what I do, but not a big motivating factor."

And one of his roomates at the academy felt that David's priorities were still in Annapolis.

"David originally chose this place because he wanted something besides basketball," the roommate said. "He stuck by his guns last summer when he could have transferred because he had made the committment originally and that is the way he is. He has a ton of pride about himself, and I mean not necessarily as a basketball player or a black person, but as an intelligent individual. A

43

diploma from here means more to him than the millions he could have made."

But with just one more year remaining for him at Annapolis, David would find it hard to avoid the questions, the publicity, and the options involving his future.

Chapter 5

Player of the Year

Before returning to school for his senior year, David got another taste of international basketball. He was a member of the United States National Team that competed in the world championships in Spain. By the time play started, David was a full seven feet tall.

The American team swept through the competition, heading for a showdown gold medal game against the Russian team. That game held more than a passing interest for basketball fans. The Russian team was anchored by a seven-footer of its own. His name was Arvidas Sabonis and many people had said that Sabonis was good enough to play in the NBA.

In the game, David took Sabonis to school. He was much quicker than the Russian, stronger off the boards, and a better shot-blocker. There was also no contest in the ability to score points. David was, by far, the superior player and he led the

United States to the gold medal. Back home, there was more talk among basketball fans about just how David would fare in the NBA against centers like Patrick Ewing and Hakeem Olajuwon.

But Navy still had first call on him, and when he reported to practice for the first time, eyes popped. David was now a full 7'1" tall and had filled out to a muscular 235 pounds. That meant he had grown a full six inches since entering the academy. The team would need every inch of him in 1986-87. Two important members of David's supporting cast, Vernon Butler and Kylor Whitaker, had graduated. And Pete Hermann had been elevated from assistant to head coach.

As assistant coach, Pete Hermann had probably communicated with David more than anyone else over the years. He knew him very well and immediately saw the change in him.

"I think the better David became, the more he felt he wanted to keep improving," the coach said. "He was obviously bigger and stronger as a senior and had played very well against the Russians at the world championships. When I spoke with him during the preseason, I asked him his goals and his answer sort of surprised me.

"He told me he wanted to be college Player of the Year. The year before, Walter Berry of St. John's had won that award, and I remembered that during his senior year Berry had come out like a guy on fire. That's what I told David. If he wanted to be Player of the Year he had to come out ready to go and be terrific. That's just what he did. He was on fire and never quieted down."

David knew from the start that his role would be a bit different on this Navy team. With Butler and Whitaker gone, so was a good deal of his support scoring. The team just didn't have the shooters to replace them and the bench was also weaker. David would be counted on to carry even more of the scoring load.

He came out firing against North Carolina State in the opener of the Tip Off Classic. Though the Wolfpack won a close victory, 86-84, David had opened the season with a big 36-point effort. His offense seemed more varied, his shooting range better. And despite his increased size and weight, he was still quicker than any other big man around.

Two games later, Navy was playing in the Cutlass Classic and going up against another tough school, Michigan State. As always, the Navy offense kept pounding the ball in to David and he continued to bring the crowd to its feet with a variety of lightning-fast offensive moves. The Spartans tried everything to stop him, then just tried to outscore him.

The game went into overtime, where David and Navy pulled it out, 91-90. When the smoke cleared David had a career high 43 points and, for good measure, 16 rebounds. He had scored almost half his team's points in a game that once again brought him national attention. The player getting the ball to David for many of his hoops was point guard Doug Wojcik. He said it was a pleasure working with the big guy.

"We had a keen sense of awareness between us," Wojcik said. "All David had to do was lift his head a little or shift his eyes toward the bucket and I'd throw him an alley-oop. Then he'd go get it and finish the play."

The 1986-87 Navy team was not unlike the teams from the two previous seasons. Unless David had an off night, the smaller schools on the schedule didn't have much of a chance. And unless David had a super night, Navy didn't have much of a chance against the traditional basketball powers. It was just a little more difficult this time around because David's supporting cast wasn't quite as good.

The pattern could be seen early in the season. Navy won easily against the likes of Yale, St. Leo, and Idaho State. But then they came up against University of Nevada-Las Vegas (UNLV) and were beaten badly, 104-79. David had 29 points, but just nine rebounds in that one. The Runnin' Rebels simply ran the Middies into the ground.

When David had an off night against Richmond, the Middies lost, 64-62. In the very next game, David made up for the off night by catching fire. He scored 45 points and grabbed 21 rebounds in a 95-70 victory over James Madison. Then there was an 83-80 loss to Drexel, a game in which David had 44 points. On that night, it wasn't enough because the other players didn't get the job done.

David also had to face more double- and triple-teaming his senior year. Forward Vernon Butler was a big 240-pound bull underneath the basket and had been a good shooter during the previous two seasons. He simply couldn't be ignored and had served as a buffer for David. Now, without Butler to worry about, defenses began sagging in on David, who would position himself back to the basket in the low post position. (The low post is the area near the basket but outside the lane, the painted strip in front of the basket.) There were even times when four defending players surrounded him on all sides. But offensively, his skills had reached such a high level that no defense could really shut him down. Even rough tactics didn't slow him down.

His biggest booster during the season was his coach, Pete Hermann. He had known David since his senior year in high school and continued to marvel at how easy it was to work with him.

"David had grown greatly as a person. He never demanded anything and always gave of himself," the coach said. "He responded to every challenge as a senior, from the big games on national television to the simple things we asked him to do in practice. It may sound corny to some people, but David is a wonderful person and was just a delight to be around all those years."

During David's senior year he was beseiged by requests for interviews, autographs, handshakes, and just about everything else. With basketball and a demanding study schedule, it wasn't always easy for him. The questions were often the same. David was asked over and over again about his future, about pro ball, and whether he would try to play part-time or wait until his five-year hitch was over.

There must have been times when David became annoyed by all this, but he always remained courteous. He answered the questions quietly and calmly, never losing his temper or his patience. Then in January, with the season still in full swing, rumors began to circulate that the Navy was about to make a decision regarding the future of David Robinson.

As it turned out, David was aware that Secretary of the Navy John Lehman was indeed about to make a ruling that would change his duty requirements after graduation. And if those requirements changed, his future as a professional basketball player might change, as well.

At first glance, the ruling seemed simple. Upon graduation, David would be commissioned as an officer in the Naval Reserve instead of the regular navy. The difference was that officers in the Naval Reserve only have to serve two years active duty instead of the five years required in the regular navy.

Did this mean David was getting special treatment? Was the navy making an exception so he would have a better chance of playing pro ball? That's how it seemed at first to many people. Another star athlete being pampered by the system. No, the Navy said. There was a good reason for the decision.

Secretary Lehman said that at 7'1" David was simply too tall to perform as an unrestricted line officer in the United States Navy. The funny part of it was that there had been a standing joke for two

50

years which said they would need a can opener to get David into a submarine. When David was asked about the ruling, he seemed happy that some kind of decision had been reached.

"Two years is better than five," he said. "I'm glad it's over and I know what my future is going to be. I've probably been more ruffled the last three days than I've ever been before. I've always felt the navy would be fair and consider what's best for me and what's best for them. Some people are going to be upset, feeling like they're making concessions for me. But half the people are going to be glad for me because they feel I'm gifted and it's not my fault that I've grown."

David had been ready to accept any ruling the navy made. He didn't ask for the reduction in duty time. Had he remained at 6'7", his height when he was admitted, and still been a superstar ballplayer, the navy would not have made the same decision. There simply aren't many seven-footers in military service, if any at all.

Doug Wojcik, for one, said that the ruling put David in a somewhat awkward situation. "He couldn't really say a whole lot about it around school," Wojcik explained. "This is an old school where you come with the object of going into the navy, and because of that, some hard-liners did not agree with the decision. But I know David was quite relieved and excited about the opportunity it gave him. But don't get the wrong idea. At the same time, David was always extremely pleased with the navy."

The ruling also raised a whole new series of questions. Would David be allowed to play part-time when he was in the reserve? That had been done before. Napoleon McCallum, who was an All-American running back at Navy, had played professional football with the Los Angeles Raiders on weekends while still on active duty.

The navy said immediately that they would release David to play in both the Pan Am Games and 1988 Olympics if he desired. That seemed to indicate they might also let him play some in the NBA. Needless to say, David was asked repeatedly about his plans, and what he wanted to do.

"As of now, I don't know what I want to do," he said. "I have to look at the details of each option and I'm not sure which I want to take. I know it would be tough to play in the NBA and be in the navy. I'll have to see which drives me more."

In basketball, being a part-time player would have some definite drawbacks. The team would constantly have to adjust and readjust. Would their center be there or would he not? Former star center Bill Walton once tried playing part-time with the San Diego Clippers while recovering from a foot injury. The foot could only take about one game a week. The experiment didn't work well. The other Clippers felt Walton's occasional presence disrupted the flow of the team.

Because talented centers like David are always at a premium in the NBA, it would be hard to see any team passing up a chance to get David's name on a contract, even a part-time one. Still, opinions varied.

Phil Johnson, coach of the Sacramento Kings, didn't think a part-time player—even a great one—would be the right thing for his team.

"David is so good," Johnson said, "but you might still be better off biting the bullet and waiting the two years for him. You could try it, but my feeling is that a part-time player would be somewhat disruptive."

Don Nelson, then coaching the Milwaukee Bucks, disagreed. "I wouldn't have any problems taking David Robinson part-time," Nelson said, "simply because he's that good. He'd still be part of your team. Sure, I'd take him now and just wait two years to get him full-time."

Listening to David, he seemed to be saying that he would be willing to play part-time in the right situation and if he could create an acceptable balance in his life.

"The NBA is definitely a full-time job," he said. "It would be tough to play and serve in the navy at the same time. But I also think that playing part-time would get me used to the scenery, the whole lifestyle for two years. The team I was on just couldn't worry about me contributing that much. They would be priming for the third year, when I'm discharged."

The decision about David playing part-time would not be made immediately. With all the hoopla surrounding the change in David's status, people had to be reminded that there was still nearly half a basketball season to play. David didn't need any more distractions.

Navy's next big test came against Kentucky, a

traditional powerhouse. The Middies would be playing the Wildcats on national television, and the game once again served to show everyone that David was not only the best collegiate big man in the entire country, but perhaps the best all-around player as well.

He came close to beating the Wildcats almost single-handedly. There wasn't anything he didn't do except maybe bring the ball upcourt. On offense, he showed all his dazzling moves against a defense that sagged all over him. He hit on a variety of jumpers, hooks, and dunks. He ran the floor the entire game, and was a one-man wrecking crew on defense.

But he couldn't overcome Kentucky's superior manpower and the Wildcats finally won the game, 80-69. But David had equalled his career high by scoring 45 points. He also grabbed 14 rebounds and blocked an amazing ten Kentucky shots.

"David Robinson is the absolute best," said one coach. "The only other college center who has come close to achieving his skill level in such a short time is Hakeem Olajuwon. But David is more versatile offensively than Olajuwon was at the same stage of his career."

David was doing it all. Against UNC-Wilmington he won the game with a clutch jump shot in the final second. Then in a game with James Madison he broke a tie with a 42-foot desperation shot at the buzzer that hit nothing but net.

"David made an unbelievable shot against James Madison," said Pete Hermann. "But he was always clutch and wanted the ball when the game was on the line. Those are the biggest things you remember as a coach."

After the loss to Kentucky, Navy went on a roll. Led by David's amazing play, the Middies won 13 straight games, which took them through the end of the regular season and then to victory in their conference tournament. They now had a 26-5 record, which was all the more incredible because, aside from David, the club just wasn't as solid as the season before. Yet that club was 27-4 at the same stage of the season, an almost identical record. The question now was whether they could go as far in the NCAA playoffs.

The Middies were once again placed in the East Regional and drew a tough bracket. Their first game would be against Michigan, and if they got by the Wolverines they'd have to face the North Carolina Tar Heels. David geared up for the final run of his college career.

Coach Hermann knew his team would have trouble with Michigan. The Wolverines played an up-tempo game, running the ball on offense and pressing on defense. That was what gave Navy the most trouble. With teams that played a slower, half-court game, David could dominate at both ends.

David had done a lot of things in four years that had surprised his coach. But nothing surprised him more than what happened in the locker room before the Michigan game. The tension was so thick it could be cut with the proverbial knife. Coach Hermann saw David sitting there, concentrating on the ball game. Suddenly, David motioned for the coach to come over. Pete Hermann thought his star was about to talk strategy.

"Instead of saying something about the game, David suddenly asked me, 'Coach, have you ever tried Tai Kwon Do?' That was a form of martial arts that he was studying. I was shocked. I just said, 'What, Dave?' And he said, 'I'm into it now and it's great. It really helps me a lot.' And here I am thinking, we're 15 minutes from taking the floor against Michigan. Why is he telling me this now? He's got to be kidding. But that was David. He loved the challenge of new things and his mind was always occupied with something."

As expected, Michigan played pressure basketball right from the opening tap. The Middies were just no match for the frenetic pace the Wolverines set. Just a few minutes into the game there was little doubt which team would win. But David Robinson was making it interesting. He was in the midst of perhaps the greatest game of his college life.

Michigan did everything right except stop David. It's doubtful any team could have stopped him on this night. Offensively, he was getting the ball, and once he had it he was scoring. The defense didn't matter. David simply made one brilliant move after another to get his shot.

When the game ended Michigan had a solid, 97-82, victory. But David had hit on 22 of 37 field goal tries, adding six free throws to close his college career with an incredible 50-point effort. Navy was eliminated, but David saw his own stock go even higher. He was truly the best in the nation.

He wound up his senior year with 903 points, an average of 28.2 points a game, third best among the nation's Division I players. He had 378 rebounds for an 11.8 average, fourth best in the country, and his 144 blocks for a 4.5 average again was a national best. Someone pointed out that both his rebounds and blocks were down from his junior year. Pete Hermann explained why.

"The blocks were probably down because teams just stopped taking it inside against him," his coach said. "They saw what happened the year before and he still led the nation anyway. Part of the reason his rebounds were down some was probably because he was asked to carry more of a load on the offensive end. There's no doubt that he just got better and better every year he was here."

Not surprisingly, David set a slew of Naval Academy records. He had become the Middies all-time scoring, rebounding, and shot-blocking leader. At the time he was also the NCAA all-time leader in blocked shots, with 516 for his career. His 207 as a junior also set a new mark, as did his 14 for a single game. This time there was no question about David being a consensus All-American. He was named on every major poll.

And he also realized the goal he had set before the season when he told his coach what he wanted to accomplish in 1986-87. David soon learned that he was an overwhelming choice as college basketball's Player of the Year.

Now he was fully ready to move on to the next phase of his life.

Chapter 6

The Road to the NBA

Once the 1986-87 season ended, basketball went on hold. David received his All-American and Player of the Year honors, then had to think about other things. First of all, he had to hit the books hard to complete his course of study at the academy. His grades had always been high and, as in a basketball game, he wanted to finish strong.

In June of 1987, he proudly received his bachelor's degree in mathematics and graduated with the rest of his class. He was now Ensign David Robinson, an officer in the United States Navy. That July, he was sent to the Navy submarine base at Kings Bay, Georgia, where he would be working as an assistant resident officer in charge of construction. In return for his services, the Navy would pay him a modest salary of $315.23 a week.

David had learned that there was no chance of him becoming a part-time NBA player during the next two years. There was a new secretary of the navy, and when the matter of David playing part-time came up, he immediately said he wouldn't permit it.

That led to a dilemma for a number of NBA teams. The 1987 draft was approaching rapidly and any team that had been thinking of using a high pick to draft David knew it would have to wait two years for his services. And that wouldn't be the only risk they were taking.

If a team used its pick to draft David and he chose not to sign with them, they would have simply wasted a pick. That's a big risk for a team to take. Waste a high number one pick and you can set your team back several years. David, on the other hand, would be the one with the options. If a team picked him, he could sign right away, then not play for two years. Or he could choose not to sign, re-enter the draft the next year, and have the same option once again.

The risk for David was that his value as a player could drop the second or third year. He wouldn't be playing much basketball in that time, so it would be more difficult for him to demand top dollar. Right now, he was the hottest hoop commodity in the country, the Player of the Year and a potential franchise center. His value was probably at its peak.

David wouldn't comment on which way he would go. "It's a great option to say that two years from now I can play with whomever I want," he said. "The big factor for me is my comfort level. I realize that wherever I go, there's going to be something I don't like, whether it's the traffic on the freeways or the smog during the summer."

The draft lottery was in effect in 1987, meaning that the weaker teams in the league, the nonplayoff clubs from the year before, would gather to determine the draft order by random selection. When the team names were drawn, the San Antonio Spurs emerged with the number one pick. The Spurs wasted no time in making their decision. To them, it was well worth the risk.

"With their number one pick, the Spurs choose David Robinson, center, United States Naval Academy," a team representative declared proudly.

It was a simple enough announcement, but it sent shock waves through San Antonio and the basketball world everywhere. Would David sign with them? Could a player who had to sit two years still command top dollar? How good would he be after a two-year layoff? At first, David wouldn't discuss his feelings.

There was little doubt that the Spurs were desperately in need of a superstar center. The team was formed in 1967 as part of the rival American Basketball Association, moved from Dallas to San Antonio in 1973, and was absorbed into the NBA when the newer league folded after the 1975-76 season.

There were several solid seasons in the late 1970s and early 1980s when San Antonio's George "Iceman" Gervin was winning scoring titles and leading the ball club. The team made it all the way to the Western Conference finals in 1982-83, but never got any further than that. Then the club began to decline. By 1986-87, when David was Mr. Basketball in the college ranks, the Spurs were last in their division, with a 28-54 record.

With talk about the franchise moving and fan support at a low ebb, the need for a David Robinson was more apparent than ever. That's why the team took a major risk in drafting him. At first, however, David woudn't commit himself.

"I just want to relax and enjoy my experience in the navy," he said.

But a short time later word leaked out that David's representatives had opened negotiations with the Spurs. David, meanwhile, received permission from the navy to join the United States team that would be playing in the Pan Am Games. With David anchoring the club, it was expected to win a gold medal. But when they were upset by Brazil in the final, the fingers pointed at David. Critics said his performance was lackluster, that he didn't play with the same desire he had at Navy. His defenders said he was simply rusty and not in game shape.

For a couple of months after that, the excitement died down. Spurs fans prepared for another lowly season and David continued to serve at Kings Bay with little fanfare. That's why the announcement that came out of San Antonio in November took everyone by surprise.

The Spurs had signed David Robinson to an eight-year contract worth a total of $26 million. David would begin playing for the Spurs in the

1989-90 season. That was still two years away, but he had already become one of the highest paid athletes in all of sports and had received the security he was looking for.

A number of people were surprised by the signing. They thought David would wait and weigh his options over the next several seasons. They also felt that he was tailor-made for one of the high-profile media centers—Chicago, New York, Los Angeles—where his good looks, articulate manner and obvious intelligence would make him a media celebrity as well as a star player. But that wasn't what David wanted.

"David needs San Antonio at this point in his life," was the way his father, Ambrose, put it. And David himself said he wanted the chance to grow in a relaxed setting. He didn't want the pressures of a New York or Los Angeles.

That's why David was willing to sign with the Spurs. He had the security of an incredible contract and the team was willing to wait two years for him. He only hoped he would be able to pay them back once he got there. He watched from a distance as the Spurs struggled through the 1987-88 season. The team finished with a 31-51 mark, barely made the playoffs, then were eliminated in three straight by the Los Angeles Lakers. Once again the fans began looking to David as a saviour.

In the summer of 1988, the Navy once again gave David permission to play basketball. This time he was allowed to try out for the United States Olympic team. To many, the presence of Robinson in the middle should have just about guaranteed a gold medal. After all, look what he had done to Arvidas Sabonis a few years earlier. He ate up the seven-foot Russian center.

David went to Europe with the team in June for some practice games. Word began filtering back that he wasn't playing well. Once again his game seemed to lack the enthusiasm and fire it usually had. Rust again? David's fans said he'd return to form by the Olympics. In a game against a woefully outclassed French team, David played 19 minutes and had just four points. He also had four fouls and four turnovers. He looked awful.

"Traditionally, I've not done well against lesser competition," David said. "But the one thing this series of games has shown me is how far I have to go and in what areas I'm hurting. My offense is way behind and I need to go to the basket more."

David continued to play poorly. It was hard to believe his game could have deteriorated so quickly. One of his teammates, Steve Kerr, didn't like the whole scenario.

"Dave's so rusty and doesn't act like he's into the games at all," Kerr explained. "I don't see how this tour does the rest of us much good because the competition is so ridiculous. But the whole trip was supposed to be for David and that kind of worries me."

David eventually made the team, though assistant coach George Raveling commented that he "hasn't played with intensity like we want him to or dominated like he can." He finally had a big game against Spain, leading everyone to think that he was finally putting it together.

"All the questions have been answered," George Raveling said.

David himself knew he had a long way to go. "I didn't feel that far behind at the Olympic trials," he said, "but the more I play and the more I see about myself, the more I notice deficiencies that I'd rather not talk about. I'm only 70 percent of where I want to be."

As it turned out, neither David nor the rest of the team played well at the Los Angeles Olympics. The United States team finished third, the worst showing ever for a U.S. Olympic basketball team. David averaged just 12 points and six rebounds a game, and many blamed him for the United States failure to win gold.

"Great centers win championships," said George Raveling.

One factor that came out later was that David just didn't get along with head coach John Thompson of Georgetown. Thompson's style is that the coach is the boss. What he says goes, no questions asked. With David's intellectual curiosity, the question "why?" was always a big part of his being. Apparently, Thompson didn't like being questioned.

"I don't permit people to question me," he said, "or else they're not on my team."

David's answer was, "He just wanted guys to run through a brick wall for him. I analyzed things. I had to, because the game was still new to me."

DAVID KLUTHO / SPORTS ILLUSTRATED

FOCUS ON SPORTS

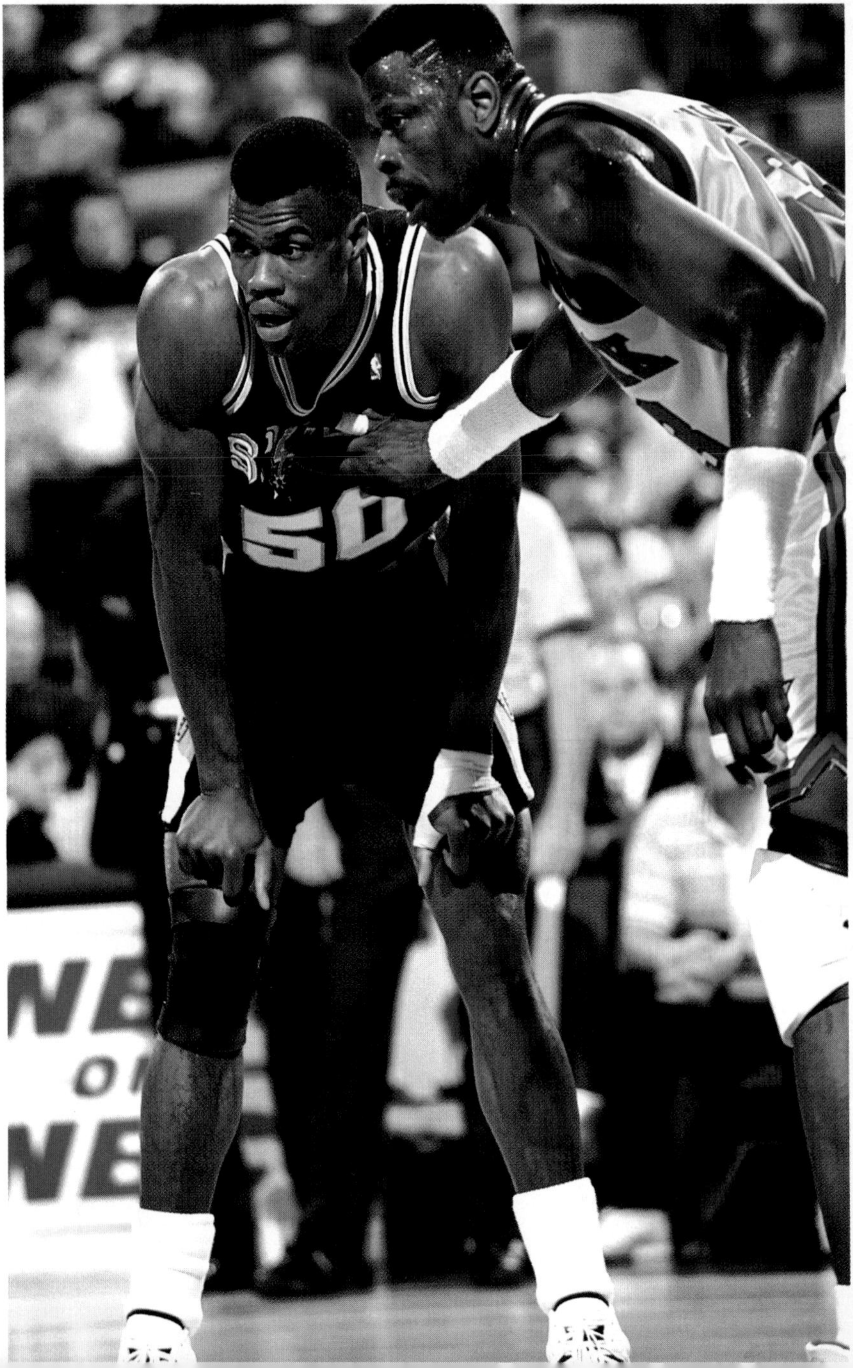

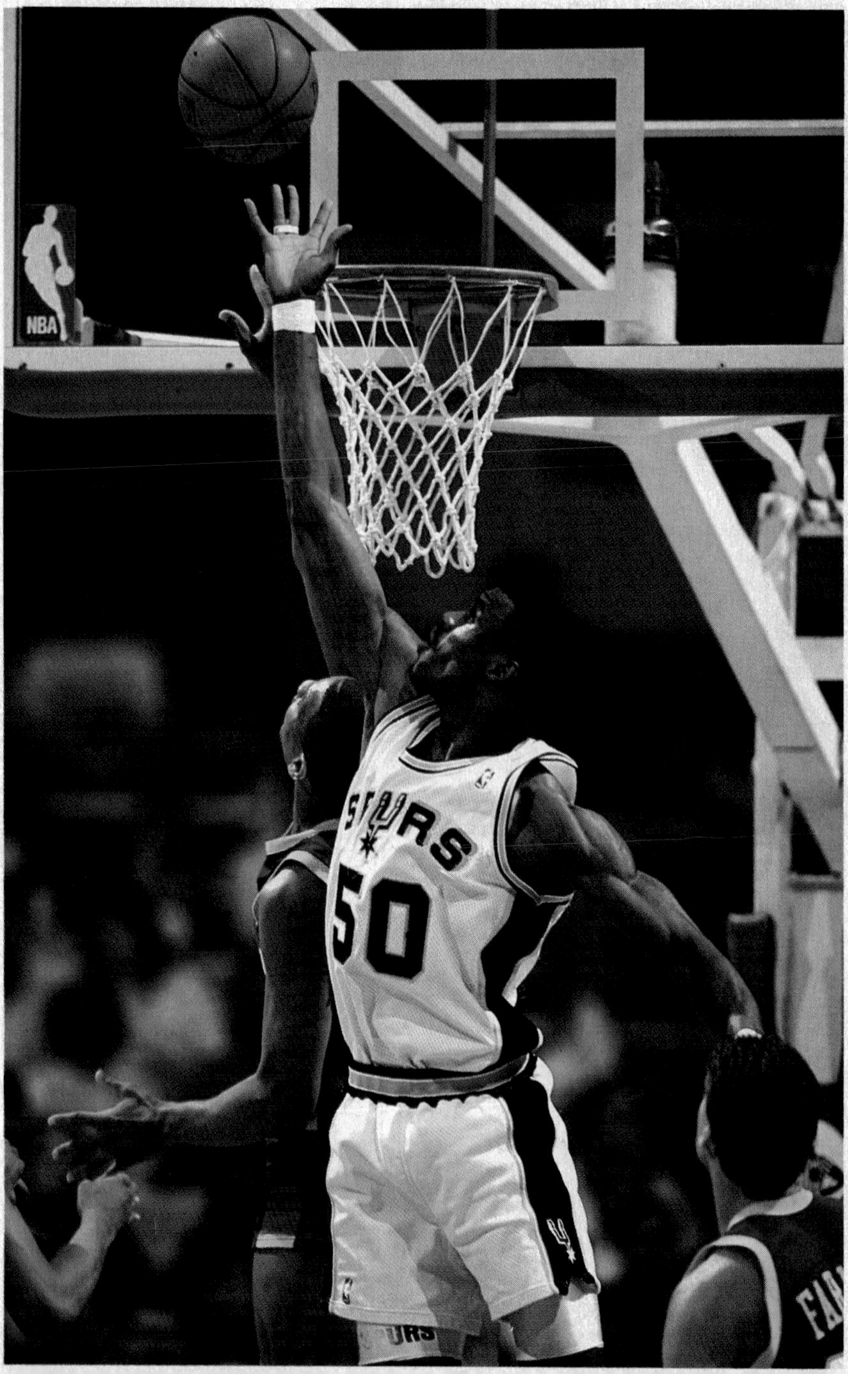

FOCUS ON SPORTS

Whatever the reason, the United States didn't win and David didn't play well. Needless to say, that raised questions about his ultimate value as a pro. Did he have the ability and the temperament to be a franchise center? Did he want it bad enough? Only time would tell.

There was still a way to go before that time would be approaching. In San Antonio, the Spurs had a new owner and a new coach. The new coach was Larry Brown, who had coached at both the college and professional level, and had been a winner everywhere. In fact, he had just come off a season where he led the University of Kansas to the national championship.

Brown took over the Spurs for the 1988-89 season and took on the challenge of making them a winner. But in his first season he coached the Spurs to a 21-61 record, the worst in team's history. Injuries and a lack of top talent made the team a weak and limited one. Brown had to rebuild quickly. The good news was that they would finally have David Robinson.

On May 19, 1989, David was discharged from the navy. He had completed his obligation and was now free to pursue a career in professional basketball. He immediately set a target date for himself. It was the night of November 4, when the Spurs would open the new season against Magic Johnson and the Los Angeles Lakers. He wanted to be ready.

"I know I'll be nervous when that day comes," David admitted. "Nervousness always shows up in my leg and my right leg will probably be going about 100 miles an hour that afternoon. I'll be so hyped up. Let's say I'm already feeling the anticipation."

David knew there was plenty of work to be done. In some ways, he felt he was at a disadvantage. But in others, he thought his naval experience might help.

"People I played with in college were out getting better and I wasn't," he said. "But I simply resolved to enjoy being in the navy, which I did. And I think that will help me in one respect. Most guys coming into the NBA have to get used to the pro game as well as to the lifestyle of being on their own. I've already had two years of being on my own, so my only adjustment will be to the NBA."

But that adjustment wouldn't be easy. As a center, David had a tougher job than if he were a point guard. He acknowledged that he had an awful lot to learn. But that's really what his whole life had been about. As he put it, "There's always something to learn."

His first stop with the Spurs was the rookie camp. Working with brand-new rookies, rookie hopefuls, and a few retreads looking for one more shot, David sharpened his game as camp progressed. In the final intrasquad game he scored 31 points, grabbed 17 rebounds, and blocked 10 shots. It was only against rookies, but he was playing with increasing confidence and a lot of hustle and desire. He certainly wasn't the laid-back player some of his Olympic teammates and coaches described.

From there he went to the Midwest Rookie Review, a round robin series of games in San Antonio between rookies from the Spurs, the Houston Rockets, the Minnesota Timberwolves, and the Denver Nuggets. Fans from San Antonio flocked to get their first glimpse of their new center. They saw David lead the Spurs rookies to a 3-0 record on the strength of 22.7 point scoring, 8.7 rebounds, and 4.3 blocks per game. He was beginning to look like the real thing.

David's basketball education and conditioning continued. He then traveled to the Southern California Summer Pro League. It's a league where play is very physical, there is not much officiating, and street rules apply. It was the kind of basketball David missed when he was a kid interested in other things. But he took to the game rapidly and led the Spurs team to six wins in seven games.

This time around he averaged 25.6 points, 6.4 rebounds and 4.2 blocks. He smiled broadly when it was announced that he had been chosen as the league's Most Valuable Player.

"I haven't felt this way in a long time," David said. "There's a new motivation for me. I love challenges and this is a new challenge. In the summer league I had fun, but also found the things I needed to work on."

As always, David was analyzing his game, trying to pinpoint strengths and weaknessses. He already felt that he had something no other NBA center could match.

"I plan to run all the time and beat my opponent

up and down the floor," he said. "When I do that, no one can do anything about it. When I run like I can, nobody can run with me."

While David was working hard to get his game back in shape, Larry Brown and the Spurs management were working to restructure the team. They made a deal with Milwaukee to get 6'9" forward Terry Cummings, a veteran with a 22.3 point career scoring average. Cummings would not only provide scoring, but also poise and leadership. He would be an excellent player to have on the front line with the rookie Robinson.

Next came the draft. This time the Spurs picked third and promptly tabbed Sean Elliott of Arizona. Elliott was a 6'8", 205-pound forward who was not only the PAC-10's (Pacific Athletic Conference) all-time scoring leader, but had just finished a season in which he was named Player of the Year.

The team also signed 6'11" Caldwell Jones, a center with 14 years' experience in the NBA. Jones had been an outstanding defensive center. At age 39, he wouldn't have a lot of playing time left, but he was the perfect guy to tutor and work with David. A final preseason deal brought veteran point guard Maurice Cheeks to the team. Cheeks was a cagey veteran who still had most of his skills at age 33. There were few better at running a ball club from the point.

So the pieces all seemed to be in place. Fans hoped the Spurs would be a much improved team from the season before. Yet with all the changes, the key still seemed to be David Robinson. No player had ever come in with more anticipation. He also seemed to be coming in with a purpose.

"I want to be one of the top four centers in the league," David said, shortly after arriving in camp. "That's what I should be, at the least. I have only one goal and that's to improve each game all year. I don't have number goals, only to rebound and contribute both offensively and defensively.

"I feel I'm ready. Two years have sometimes seemed like ten. The closer I get, the more anticipation I feel."

So did his coaches, teammates, and fans.

Chapter 7

Rookie
Sensation

There was little doubt that David had come to training camp in shape and ready to play. He looked bigger, stronger, and quicker than the All-American navy version. He said he had spent a great deal of time during his two-year navy hitch working with weights. He concentrated on both strength and agility.

At 7'1", 235 pounds, there wasn't an ounce of fat on him. Naturally long and lean, David still had thin legs and just a 33-inch waist. But now his shoulders and arms were very muscular. His biceps could almost be described as huge. It was a look he didn't have at Navy. David knew that play in the NBA was very rough and physical. He wanted to be ready.

With David and the other new players the team had brought in, the Spurs looked like a much different team, one that was ready to win. And Coach Brown felt he had the right players to blend with the rookie Robinson.

"Having Maurice Cheeks and Terry Cummings is the big thing," Brown said. "The worst thing that could have happened to David would have been to come into the league and not have guys like that around. Caldwell Jones will be a tremendous help to him, as well."

In the preseason it was apparent that both David and his new teammates were going to be formidable. As he had predicted, he could run better than just about any pivotman in the league. He no longer ran out of gas at the end of games. Cheeks was still Cheeks, one of the steadiest point guards in recent years. Cummings was just a notch below superstar level. Young Elliott had signed late. He would not be an instant star, but certainly would contribute. Second year shooting guard Willie Anderson also had star potential.

Finally, the big night arrived. The 1989-90 version of the Spurs took the court to a huge ovation from the 15,868 fans who jammed the HemisFair Arena in San Diego to see the Spurs meet the powerful Lakers in the season opener. As for star quality, the two players the fans most wanted to see were Magic Johnson and the rookie, David Robinson. David got a rousing standing ovation when he was introduced with the starting lineup. It was an ovation that had been on hold for two years.

When David took the floor in an NBA game for the first time, he knew he would be the center of attention in more ways than one. All rookies get tested. Rookies with a big reputation are tested even more. And those tests are usually in the form of physical intimidation. Three times in the first period alone, David was fouled hard as he worked for position under the hoop. The veterans were trying to push him out of the way.

It took less than a full quarter of action for the Laker forwards to realize they weren't playing against an ordinary rookie center who would go on to be nothing more than a journeyman player. David was holding his position, drawing the fouls, then calmly hitting his free throws with a soft, left-handed touch.

The game stayed close right through the second period. The Lakers had been runners-up to Detroit the season before and had won three of the previous four NBA Finals before that. Yet they couldn't pull away from the Spurs. Late in the third period San Antonio had a 72-70 lead. The Lakers had the ball with the great Magic Johnson running the show, as usual.

Magic brought the ball over the center line, his eyes scanning the court quickly. Any small opening and he could whip a pass to a teammate for a hoop. Only this time he sensed a hole in the middle of the defense. He accelerated and drove down the lane looking to go right to the hoop. As he floated to the hoop, the huge form of David Robinson came soaring over from the side, hand in the air. Just as Magic released the ball, David was there to bat it away. The crowd went absolutely ballistic.

It was his first professional block. Not only did he get it against one of the all-time greats, but it also served to turn the game around. San Antonio went on a 6-0 run after David's rejection and went on to win the game, 106-98. Not only had the Spurs won their opener, but they had beaten one of the best teams in the league.

But a victory for the new Spurs wasn't the only sensational debut that night. David had stepped right into the NBA and had made it his personal stage. His first pro game ever produced 23 points, a team high, including 11 of 14 from the foul line. He also led both clubs with 17 rebounds. One of the players he impressed was Magic Johnson, victim of his first blocked shot.

"Some rookies are never really rookies," Magic told reporters after the game. "Robinson is one of them."

From the Magic man, that was the ultimate compliment. To him, David Robinson was already a player the Lakers and everyone else would have to reckon with. And when the reporters gathered around David in the Spurs' locker room, he answered their questions in a way that had some of the writers running for the dictionary.

"My job is to keep opponents from taking the ball to the hoop with impunity," he said. "All the attention I've received is a little bit embarrassing. All I'm trying to do is make my place in the league."

It took David one game to erase memories of the Pan Am Games and the Olympics and silence all those people who had taken pot shots at him in the two years since he graduated from the academy. But one game does not make a career. Two nights later, the Spurs were beaten by the Portland Trailblazers, 108-104. But David was outstanding again, hauling in 18 rebounds. Soon after, he scored 27 points and added 13 rebounds in a loss to the Utah Jazz, then had 28 points and 11 boards in a big victory over the Denver Nuggets.

With nine new players on the roster, the Spurs were still getting to know each other. But by the end of November the team had an 8-5 record and was definitely much better than the 21-61 team of a year earlier. The question was how much better. Cheeks and Cummings had fit in well. Willie Anderson was looking like the real thing, a player. Elliott was struggling a bit, but his talent was undeniable. As for David Robinson, well, he was already looking like a superstar and a franchise center.

Franchise centers are always compared to those who came before them. With the NBA there is something called the lineage. The line of great centers. It started with big George Mikan, a scoring star in the 1940s and 1950s. Mikan was 6'10", a giant in his day, although a limited player compared to those today. But he led the old Minneapolis Lakers to five NBA titles.

The center who revolutionized the game was Bill Russell of the Boston Celtics. Russell was probably just a tall 6'9", but he was very athletic and even more tenacious. He joined the Celtics in 1956-57 and was the first great defensive center, a rebounder and shot-blocker who would undoubtedly still be a superstar in today's game. With Russell in the lineup, the Celtics won 11 NBA championships in 13 years, an incredible run.

In 1959-60, Goliath came into the league. He was Wilt Chamberlain, a 7'1" center who was the first real giant at the position. Wilt was also skilled, a tremendous scorer and rebounder who could do it all. His battles with Russell were epic, and while he didn't always play with great teams, he owns a pair of championship rings and a lot of records.

Then in 1969-70, a 7'2" center named Lew Alcindor joined the Milwaukee Bucks. Alcindor had been a great college center at UCLA. Two years later he changed his named to Kareem Abdul-Jabbar and embarked on a long career with Milwaukee and Los Angeles. He's the NBA's all-time leading scorer (ahead of Wilt) and helped his teams to six world titles.

Those are still considered the big four in the lineage. Bill Walton might have joined the group, but repeated foot injuries limited his effectiveness and shortened his career. Others came close. Centers like Nate Thurmond, Bob Lanier, Artis Gilmore, Willis Reed, and Walt Bellamy all had superstar tools, but are considered a notch below the big four.

When David entered the NBA in 1989-90, there were two young centers in the league considered to have the potential to become part of the lineage. They were Patrick Ewing of the New York Knicks and Hakeem Olajuwon of the Houston Rockets. Olajuwon started playing in the NBA in 1984-85, Ewing a year later. They were just two and three years older than David. Neither had yet made his mark, other than having obvious talent. The field was open for David to join them.

By December, the Spurs were starting to look even stronger. In fact, with David in the middle and the other new players fitting in, the team was beginning to look like one of the better clubs in the league. The turnaround from the year before was amazing. During December alone the club won 11 of 13 games and took over first place in the Midwest Division of the Western Conference.

After 26 games, the Spurs had a surprising 19-7 record. A year earlier, the team was just the opposite, 7-19, after 26 games. Professional ball clubs usually don't rebuild that quickly. However, with a dominant center and a few good supporting players, teams can win. Look what David had done at Navy with a slightly-better-than-mediocre supporting cast.

Terry Cummings also played great ball in December. In fact, he was NBA Player of the Week from the 17th to the 24th with a string of high-scoring games. David was named Rookie of the Month for the second month in a row. The things he was doing on the court were attracting attention everywhere.

"He has the talent all us big guys only hope and dream for," said teammate Caldwell Jones, who had played against many top centers. "No other big guy I've ever seen is anywhere as quick and fast as David. That's what really sets him apart."

A number of opposing players refused to look at

David in terms of his being a rookie or as a potentially great player. They felt they were already seeing the real thing.

"There's no *gonna-be* about it," said Mark Acres of the Orlando Magic. "David is a great player right now."

The Spurs' pace slowed somewhat in January. That was to be expected. But there were still highlights. On January 12, the Spurs whipped the Boston Celtics, 97-90. What made it a highlight was that the game was played in Boston Garden, where San Antonio hadn't won in 20 tries. By the end of the month the team was 29-13, and David was Rookie of the Month for a third straight time.

In the eyes of many, it had taken David just three months of NBA play to reach the same level as Ewing and Olajuwon. Considering that he was coming back after a two-year layoff, that made his sensational play even more amazing. He was asked repeatedly if the pro game was what he expected, and how he had adjusted so quickly.

"It's a physical game and a challenging one," David said, "but that's pretty much what I expected. Up here you've got to protect your own and that means even making your fouls count. Sometimes there are guys hanging on you every play, doing anything to stop your shot. It isn't easy trying to be great with the kind of competition we have around the league. The easiest way to get up for every game is to keep winning."

David also said that by having to wait two years to enter the NBA, he came in wanting to succeed very badly. "This is a tough league and there are times when you just want to say 'I quit' and not play anymore," David said. "But I just think about the time I spent working out in the gym by myself, which made me realize how much I missed playing the game. I watched a lot on television and I'd see guys I played with in college and played against in college. They were in the NBA and I wasn't. That was really hard."

But he was there now. In a game against the Knicks, he outplayed Patrick Ewing in the final minutes to give the Spurs a close win. During those tense closing moments, David hit a clutch, fallaway jumper over Ewing, used his quickness to pick off a pass intended for the Knick center, then rejected a Ewing shot off a drive. Everyone was noticing just how much he was accomplishing in his first months in the league.

Charles Barkley, the outstanding forward then playing with the Philadelphia 76ers and one of the most outspoken players in the league, pulled no punches when talking about David. "He's going to be a monster," Barkley said. "David can do it all— play defense, shoot, rebound, and block shots. Plus, he's the fastest big man I've ever played against."

One of the other great big men, Hakeem Olajuwon, said David was already a great player. "He's quick, he's fast, and he's strong," Hakeem said. "For a rookie, he plays with a great deal of confidence. He doesn't hesitate."

By the end of January the Spurs had the fourth

best record in the league. David was averaging 23.3 points a game, which was tenth in the league. He was grabbing 11.4 rebounds a game, fourth best behind Olajuwon, Barkley, and Charles Oakley of the Knicks. And only Olajuwon and Ewing had blocked more shots.

That February he was named to the Western Conference squad for the NBA All-Star Game. Playing backup to starter Olajuwon, David scored 15 points and grabbed 10 rebounds in 25 minutes of action. The East won the game, 130-113, but David had impressed even more people with his stellar play.

"I played with the best there is and did okay," he said, after the game. "I was a little nervous before the game, but felt good and gained confidence after I got in. Now I just want to go back and dominate like I should in the second half of the season."

There were some nights when David didn't dominate and control the game. Every once in a while he seemed to have a lapse of concentration. There was one game with Orlando when, for some reason, David just stayed at the defensive end for ten San Antonio possessions. And they weren't even fast breaks. Did he get tired? It didn't happen too often, but even David found it difficult to explain.

"Sometimes I just find myself watching," he said, "kind of spaced out. I just don't force myself to go down and get in the action. But don't worry, when it happens Coach Brown lets me know about it."

It's difficult for any rookie to come into the NBA after playing a 30- or 35-game college schedule and suddenly have to play 82 games, plus the playoffs. Some rookies hit the so-called "wall" near the end of the season, and their performance drops off. Others just find it hard to go all out night after night, week after week, month after month.

Coach Brown did stay on David's case. Always a great motivator, he constantly prodded his rookie center to work harder and harder.

"He can be in the Hall of Fame someday," the coach said. "But when I see Patrick Ewing or Hakeem Olajuwon play, I know David isn't there yet. He's got to decide how badly he wants it, how good he wants to be. He's trying, but I don't know if it will ever happen."

That was Brown's way of challenging David, daring him to be great. Both the team and the big guy continued to play well in February. Then the club announced a surprise trade. They sent veteran point guard Cheeks to the Knicks in exchange for Rod Strickland, a second-year point guard who was a backup in New York but a player with enormous talent and potential.

Going for the younger player might have been a risk. But the team won four of its first five with Strickland in the lineup. By March they were doing so well that there were a couple of very important milestones in sight. For one thing, an 11-5 record in March brought the club 27 more wins than the year before.

The biggest one-season turnaround in NBA

history belonged to the Boston Celtics of 1979-80. That was the year Larry Bird joined the team and the Celts finished 32 games better than the year before. The Spurs had a chance to break that league mark. They also had a chance to top the team record of 53 wins in a season, set by the 1982-83 Spurs squad.

There were a number of reasons for the Spurs reversal of form. But even the critical Larry Brown admitted the biggest reason was the arrival of David Robinson. "What's happened is that in one season this has become David's team," the coach said. "He is its heart and soul. I'm not sure he realizes that yet, because everything has happened so quickly. But the more he grows into that role, the better he'll become and the better the team will become."

To David's credit, he continued to play outstanding ball. He never hit the imaginary wall, which can sap the strength from a rookie. In fact, the team won their final seven games to finish the season at 56-26. They not only won the Midwest Division, but also completed the greatest one-year turnaround in NBA history, finishing a full 35 games better than the year before.

There was also no doubt that David had played the greatest role in the rise in the team's fortunes. His rookie season had already placed him among the upper echelon of NBA centers. He finished the season tenth in the league in scoring with a 24.3 average. His 983 rebounds and 12.0 average placed him second to Olajuwon in that category, and his 3.89 blocks per game placed him third in rejections.

As good as David was, he didn't do it alone. Cummings averaged 22.4 points, Anderson 15.7, and Strickland 14.2 after arriving from New York. The Spurs now got ready for the playoffs. In the first round they would be meeting the Denver Nuggets in a best-of-five series. But before that even started, it was announced that David Robinson had been named NBA Rookie of the Year.

That came as no surprise. David was considered a shoo-in for that prize. Some thought he should get even more than that. Charles Barkley continued to be one of David's biggest boosters.

"You have to give Robinson credit," Sir Charles said. "He has turned things around for the Spurs. If you are judging by which player has improved his team the most, you would have to say that David Robinson is the league's Most Valuable Player."

That prize would go to Magic Johnson. But David had surpassed most people's expectations. He was pleased with his season so far, and by his top rookie prize. But he also took pains to remind people that basketball was a team game.

"I'm sure people are surprised that I've done so much so fast," he told reporters. "But it counts more that the team has also played well. I think any player would tell you that individual accomplishments help your ego, but if you don't win, it makes for a very, very long season."

Chapter 8

Keeping It Going

Playoff basketball in the NBA is almost a whole different game. Everything becomes more difficult. Defenses toughen, the intensity level rises, and everybody goes all out. After all, once a team is eliminated there is a long summer to think about things. Only one team can win, but many try.

The Spurs were favored over the Nuggets in the first round. Denver, 43-39 in the regular season, was a run-and-shoot type of team that didn't put much emphasis on defense. It was a fun game for the fans, but one that didn't produce the desired results against the better teams in the league.

Sure enough, the well-rounded Spurs had no problem dropping the Nuggets in three straight high-scoring games. But the next round wouldn't be easy. San Antonio had to meet the Portland Trailblazers in a best-of-seven series. The Blazers were 59-23 in the regular season and had a superstar of their own, forward Clyde "the Glide" Drexler.

Portland won the first game easily, 107-94. None of the Spurs looked good. David, in fact, had one of his poorer games of the season, finishing with just nine points and nine rebounds. It was a humbling experience for him.

"Those kinds of games just serve as reminders," he said. "Sometimes it's so easy to forget what you need to do, play defense and rebound, and be active defensively. Anybody who's seen me play all year knows I don't play like that all the time."

When Portland won the second game, 122-112, Coach Brown read his team the riot act. He chided David for playing too soft inside and told Strickland to protect the ball. The point guard had committed 12 turnovers in the first two games. And he lit into Cummings for not playing up to standards set during the regular season.

Now the series shifted from Portland to the Hemis-Fair Arena, and that seemed to serve as a wake-up call for the Spurs. They won game three easily, 121-98, as David scored 28 points and blocked eight shots. David also led the way in a 115-105 victory in Game 4 that tied the series.

"I think we're starting to play the way we like to play," said David. "We're playing more aggressively. Our guards are up on people and we're doing the fundamental things."

The rest of the series was a battle. Game 5 went into double overtime before Portland pulled out a 138-132 victory. San Antonio evened it again in the sixth game, winning, 112-97, and setting up a seventh and decisive game at Portland. The winner would be heading for the conference finals.

This seventh game was closely fought from the opening tap. It was a typical playoff struggle, very physical. Baskets came hard. At the end of regulation it was again tied. The overtime period was just as tight. Finally, with the score tied and just 30 seconds left, San Antonio had the ball again. Strickland brought it downcourt and for some reason tried an over-the-head blind pass. It was picked off by the Blazers who broke upcourt and scored. A last-second free throw made the final 108-105. The Spurs were eliminated.

David's playoff numbers were amazingly close to his regular season stats. In ten games he averaged 24.3 points, 12 rebounds, and four blocks. But they meant nothing because the team had lost the game.

With the season now over, people could stand back and look at what David had accomplished. There were more honors. He was a member of the All-Rookie Team and made third team All-NBA (behind Olajuwon and Ewing). He was also a second team All-Defensive Team choice and won the Schick Award as Player of the Year.

There was also a system used at the time to measure a player's efficiency. Called the TENDEX ratings, it was based on ten statistical categories. The ratings were released each month, then put together for the entire season. It came as no surprise when the Chicago Bulls' Michael Jordan received the highest rating of .871. But tied for second were Karl Malone of Utah and David

Robinson. Each had an .854 rating. Olajuwon was next at .851, with Ewing following with an .829.

What did it all mean? Maybe nothing. But if the TENDEX was accurate, David graded out as the best center in the league, and was close to being the top player.

During his rookie year, David's reputation grew. He was polite and patient with reporters and interviewers. Never a one-dimensional person, he was willing to talk about things other than basketball. He wasn't just another jock. Because of his combination of talent and intelligence, he was a natural to become a league and commercial spokesperson. The image presented to the public was that of an intelligent, clean-cut athlete with many off-court interests.

But as with everything else he did, David thought about his off-court activities very carefully. He wanted a positive image. Many athletes today feel they shouldn't be role models, that parents must take the responsibility for raising their kids. That may be true, but David felt that a highly visible athlete like himself did have a responsibility to the public.

"I don't think a lot of guys take it [their image as role models] as seriously as they should," he said. "But to me it's very important. The influence you can have on kids is one of the best things about the position I'm in, and I spend a lot of time with them. I go out and talk to as many kids as I can, trying to help them and give them a little boost."

Commercially, David picked up a new nickname—Mr. Robinson, again playing on his nice-guy image.

"The 'Mr. Robinson' persona is perfect for him because he is such a nice guy off the court," said Melinda Gable, a spokesperson for the shoe company David represented.

Mr. Robinson would never fully catch on as a nickname. Before long, David would get another nickname that better suited his background and the way he played the game. He would become known as "the Admiral." An admiral is the highest-ranking naval officer, the equivalent of a general in the army. David was like an admiral on the court.

After a busy off-season, David rejoined his teammates for the 1990-91 campaign. The starting five remained intact from the season before, though some of the role players had changed. Veteran swingman Paul Pressey, who played guard and forward, was a valuable addition. Because of the great turnaround of the year before and the sensational year David had produced, there were some who felt the Spurs had a chance to win the NBA title.

Injuries were a problem early in the season. Willie Anderson had a stress fracture in his leg and would miss three weeks. Strickland also had a leg injury, but came back after just three games. When David averaged 30.5 points on 63.6 percent shooting in the first four games, it looked as if he was ready to have a monster season.

He continued to play well in the early going. Against a very good Phoenix team he scored 40 points, had 14 rebounds, and blocked five shots. His performance prompted the Phoenix Suns' coach Cotton Fitzsimmons to say, "He's the greatest impact player the league has seen since Kareem Abdul-Jabbar." Fitzsimmons added that he felt Robinson had already surpassed Michael Jordan, Magic Johnson, and Larry Bird as the game's most imposing player. "They're all MVP's," he said. "This guy is more."

But praise doesn't win championships. Still, many thought the Spurs would win the division in a walk, especially when Anderson was healthy again. By the end of December the club was in first place, and along with Portland, Boston, Chicago, and Detroit, was considered one of the five best teams in the league.

In a big December game against Houston, the Spurs eked out a 96-95 victory. The statistics for the two big men were very interesting. Houston's Olajuwon had 20 points, 14 rebounds, and three blocks. David scored 18, grabbed 13 boards and had eight blocks.

"If those two are dead-even now, then I'm thrilled," said Coach Brown. "Olajuwon is in his seventh season while David's only been in the league for 100 games. But I really feel that David is different from any center. He has unbelievable speed. I remember when Kareem would dribble to half-court and everybody in the Forum would stand up. I've seen this kid dribble the length of the floor as if he were a guard."

For awhile, it looked as if only injuries could

stop the Spurs. When Anderson finally returned, Cummings went down with a bad knee. Then reserve forward Sidney Green was lost for four to six weeks with bone spurs in his ankle. But the better teams have to play through that. Only if a dominant center is lost does a team usually crumble. The Spurs knew there was no way they could replace David.

The Admiral continued to play well. When he landed with 35 points and 16 rebounds against the Hawks, longtime Atlanta superstar Dominique Wilkens commented, "They can talk about Ewing and Olajuwon, but I see David doing things they can't do."

It seemed that any time David had a big game, the opposing coach marveled at the things he could do on the court. When he scored 31 points in a 14-point win over the Denver Nuggets, Denver coach Paul Westhead noted that 24 of David's points came on dunks. "Robinson turned things around almost single-handedly," Westhead said. "He was certainly in the middle of a dunkathon. On a couple of plays he blocked a shot, outletted the ball, filled the lane, and finished off with a dunk. Most guys just block and outlet, but David is double jeopardy."

By All-Star Game time, David had the highest TENDEX rating in the league. He was named the starting center on the West squad and was the leading vote getter in the conference. Olajuwon was out with an eye injury, while David's numbers were all above Ewing's. Many were calling him the top pivotman in the game after just a season and a half. In the All-Star Game he scored 16 points in 18 minutes of action.

Shortly after the midpoint of the season the injury jinx struck again. Strickland and Cummings went down a second time, both with broken hands. Then the Spurs had another potential problem. The United States attacked military bases in Iraq and was sending ground troops to that country. The Persian Gulf War had begun. Since David was still in the Naval Reserve, he would have to go if his unit was called.

David said immediately that he would certainly go if called. His unit would probably be assigned to the Naval Facilities Engineering Command in Washington. As it turned out, his unit wasn't called, but because of his U.S. Naval Academy background, he was probably asked about the war more than any other professional athlete in the country. It was a highly personal situation for him because a number of his former friends and classmates from the academy were in the heat of the action.

"The whole thing was pretty intense for me," he said. "When I turned on the news and heard the guys on the first planes had left that morning for a bombing run over Baghdad, my stomach just dropped. I imagined those guys must be scared to death. The whole thing made playing basketball seem insignificant."

But as insignificant as it might be, the games had to go on. In late February David took over the league lead in rebounding from the injured

Olajuwon. The Spurs struggled a bit in March as injuries continued to take a toll. In mid-March, however, David still had the highest TENDEX rating in the league.

At that point in the season, the Spurs had compiled a record of 21-5 when all five starters were healthy. By late March, all five starters were back in the lineup and the team drove to the finish. They wound up with a 55-27 mark, one victory less than the year before, but good enough to win the division by one game over Utah and three over Houston.

"I'm very proud of this team," said Coach Brown. "With all the injuries and everything else that's happened, we've done as well, if not better, than we could have expected."

David finished the regular season with a 25.6 scoring average, making him ninth in the league. He was the leader in rebounds with 13 per game, and second in blocks with a 3.90 average. He was also ninth in field goal percentage, shooting at a 55.2 percent clip. That made him the only player in the league to crack the top ten in four different categories.

It was no surprise when David was named to the All-NBA First Team and also to the All-Defensive Team. He also won the Schick Award for the second consecutive year. But he would trade all that for an NBA title, and in the first round of the playoffs the team faced the Golden State Warriors in a best-of-five series.

The Warriors weren't pushovers. They were a well-coached and talented team that happened to lack a dominant center. In Chris Mullin, Mitch Richmond, and Tim Hardaway, however, they had three outstanding scorers. On a good night the Warriors were capable of driving any team to distraction.

Jim Peterson, one of the Warriors' journeyman centers, said coach Don Nelson wanted to try to take David out of his game. "Coach wanted to go with more mobile guys and keep David guessing on the defensive end," Peterson said. "He wanted to make sure this wasn't a 'big guy' series."

Would the strategy work? It didn't look that way in the first game. San Antonio beat Golden State at their own game and simply outscored them, 130-121. Then in the next two games, things changed suddenly. The Spurs had trouble coping with the Warriors' speed and mobility. Golden State won both games, 111-98 and 109-106. Now the Spurs were on the brink of an embarrassing first-round elimination.

Through three games David had 85 points and 40 rebounds. He was shooting 70 percent from the field. But in Game 4, David's offense fell off. He scored just 18 points and the balanced Warriors attack again wore down the Spurs. Golden State won, 110-97, sending the Spurs home with an early exit. David didn't take the loss easily.

"We just let them get aggressive and take the game away from us," he said. "I have to take a lot of responsibility for this team. I like to think I have an impact on the team, so I like to play well in these games. It's very disappointing."

It was quickly pointed out that both Ewing and Olajuwon also saw their teams eliminated in the first round. So all three super-centers were out of the playoffs. In fact, Detroit had won the last two NBA titles with journeyman Bill Laimbeer in the middle, and the Chicago Bulls would take the crown in 1990-91 with the aging Bill Cartwright in the middle. Maybe Charles Barkley was right when he said, "You can't win with one guy anymore. You need a supporting cast. Coaching is too good these days to let one big superstar beat you."

Maybe the game was changing a bit, or maybe the Spurs just didn't have enough of a supporting cast. David had certainly established himself after just two seasons. But with all his outside interests and his desire to learn new things, some wondered if he might not tire of the game. Or would he continue to improve and keep the fires burning inside, the kind of fire that can only be satisfied by a championship—or several championships?

Chapter 9
The Quest Continues

Though his major goal was a championship for the Spurs, David continued to do other things with his life. He felt he had to maintain a balance. He wouldn't be happy if basketball was the only thing in his world. There were times when he was criticized for it. Even his coach wondered if he was focused enough on basketball.

"Look at a guy like Magic Johnson," David said in his defense. "He's been all basketball for so long and now he's starting to do other things. People pat him on the back for that and tell him it's great that he's starting to expand his horizons."

David's horizons had been expanding for a long time. During his second season in the league he taught himself how to play the saxophone. It was something that enabled him to be creative and relax at the same time, a much needed diversion from the rigors of NBA life.

"I'm better on the piano," he said of his musical

endeavors, "but with the sax I feel so much more creative, so much freer. If I hear something, I can generally play it just by its sound. No reading notes."

But he didn't confine his off-court activities to his own development. He still respected the importance and value of education. During January of 1991 David became involved with the I Have a Dream Foundation. He adopted the entire fifth grade class at Gates Elementary School in San Antonio. He donated $124,000 to the foundation. His donation and the interest it earns will eventually provide each of the 90 students in the class with a $2,300 scholarship to attend college.

Marie Goforth, who was the foundation chairperson, was impressed by the degree of David's involvement. "Apart from the fact that he's a tremendous basketball player," she said, "David Robinson is a tremendous human being."

Perhaps the person most critical of David Robinson the basketball player was David Robinson the person. Despite becoming an All-NBA selection in just his second season and being praised up and down by rival coaches and players, David felt there were still holes in his game.

"If you're going to be a great musician, you have to have all the basics down and go from there," he said. "But with basketball, I don't really think I have all the basics down yet. There are still so many things I feel I need to learn. My effort and athletic ability help me overcome some of the things I don't do as well right now. But soon I am going to be a lot better."

And while he was already one of the top scorers in the league, he felt his offense was still lacking. His jump shot wasn't always reliable and many of his points still came on dunks.

"I do so much better in transition and when I'm driving the ball to the basket," he said. "When I go into a game, I think, 'Run, David, move your feet.' I really don't have anything past that. I found at times last year that I needed a go-to move in certain half-court scoring situations and I didn't have it. I definitely think it would be a big, big advantage if I had one."

David was saying that many of his points came off the transition game, when the team was running. Even the short jumpers he took came on transition. When the team had to set up in the half-court and run plays, he wasn't as effective. He had scored at Navy on a variety of turnaround jumpers and hooks, but he wasn't doing that as much in the NBA.

In addition, playoff basketball is so physical that it often comes down to more of a half-court game. That, in part, could have explained the Spurs' early exits from the playoffs, especially the 1990-91 loss to the Warriors. So David still looked to improve his game when the 1991-92 season rolled around.   There were no major changes in the ball club's makeup as the new season got underway. Veteran forward Antoine Carr added some muscle underneath. The other changes were minor. At first it seemed like the same old Spurs. With David leading the way, the ball club had a

10-3 record in November and were apparently headed for another fine season.

But in December and January the team began to lose more. They weren't dominating and weren't looking like one of the league's elite, despite David's continued fine play. On January 19, Willie Anderson went down with yet another stress fracture in his fragile left shin. Two days later, the club was hit by a bombshell. Larry Brown asked to be relieved of his duties as head coach. The team was 21-17 and Brown felt he couldn't take them any further.

The rest of the season was something of a struggle. The Spurs' vice-president of basketball operations, Bob Bass, took over the team and coached the rest of the way. The team picked up the pace a bit and got back in the race for the divisional crown. They were 21-9 under Bass when, on April 1, their season effectively all but ended.

That's when David had to leave the lineup with the first real injury of his career. He suffered a torn ligament in his left hand, his shooting hand, and opted for immediate surgery. His season was over. Without the Admiral in the lineup, the Spurs limped home with a record of 47-35 for the year. It was still good enough for second place in the division. Without David, the club was eliminated from the playoffs in three straight games by the Phoenix Suns.

Despite missing the final 14 games of the year and the ensuing playoffs, David received another slew of honors when the season ended. In 68 games, he averaged 23.2 points, 12.2 rebounds, and 4.5 blocks. He was seventh in scoring, fourth in rebounding, and first in blocked shots. He was also fifth in steals, with 158, and sixth in field goal percentage. That made him the just the third player in NBA history to be among the top ten in five categories. The last to do it before him was the great Larry Bird of the Celtics.

When the season ended, he was an All-NBA first team selection once again, a member of the All-Defensive Team, and he was named NBA Defensive Player of the Year. At first glance, it would appear that David was close to the top of his game, ready to jump to the head of the class of NBA centers. But the Spurs' repeated playoff failures and some personnel shifts in 1992-93 would suddenly change things. David was about to embark on the most crucial period of his basketball life.

But before that, David had a very interesting summer. He became part of the Dream Team, a group of NBA stars chosen to represent the United States at the 1992 Summer Olympics, held in Barcelona, Spain. It was the first time that NBA players were allowed to represent the U.S. at the Olympics, and the team that made the trip might have been the strongest basketball all-star team ever assembled.

In addition to David, there was Magic Johnson, Larry Bird, Michael Jordan, Patrick Ewing, Karl Malone, Clyde Drexler, Scottie Pippen, Chris Mullin, Charles Barkley, John Stockton, and a collegian, Christian Laettner. There was little doubt about the outcome, but all the NBA players enjoyed the experience.

David, of course, had played with the 1988 Olympic team, a college-dominated outfit that took a bronze in Los Angeles. He was then still in the navy and had shouldered much of the blame for the team's failure to win gold. This was different. The Dream Teamers were the most sought-after celebrities in Barcelona, and David and his teammates had the chance to talk with athletes from many different countries.

On the court it was a walkover. In the quarterfinals the United States whipped Puerto Rico, 115-77. Then in the semis, the Dream Team easily topped Lithuania, 127-76. And in the gold medal game, the U.S. beat a very good Croatian team, 117-85. All the players split playing time evenly. David averaged 9.0 points and 4.1 rebounds in the eight games and returned home with the gold medal he hadn't won in 1988.

Prior to the start of the NBA season it looked as if David had pretty much taken control of his entire life. He even had his immediate family playing major roles in his off-court endeavors. His father and mother had moved to San Antonio, where they were running the David Robinson Group, a management and investment company, part of which dealt with the marketing of David as a sports superstar.

Then in November of 1992, David and his wife, Valerie, created the David Robinson Foundation. David, always a deeply religious person, described the foundation as a "Christian organization whose mission is to support programs which address the spiritual needs of the family." Since its creation, the foundation has donated hundreds of thousands of dollars to help achieve its goals.

"This is something I've wanted to do for a long time," David said. "Having Valerie working with me just made it much easier to get off the ground. We have high hopes that the foundation will be able to provide help to those who need it for years to come."

On the basketball front, however, things were not quite so settled. In the space of several months, the face of the team had changed dramatically, starting with the coach. It was announced long before the season started that the new coach would be Jerry Tarkanian, a name familiar to basketball fans, but a shocker nevertheless.

Tarkanian was the longtime coach at the University of Nevada at Las Vegas, where he turned out winning teams, developed a number of future NBA stars, and won a national championship. But "Tark the Shark," as he was called, had no pro coaching experience. Many felt he would have a difficult time adjusting his style to deal with the pro players and NBA game.

In addition, there were many new faces to work into the lineup. Both Terry Cummings and Willie Anderson would be out with injuries when the season began. Cummings tore up a knee in July and would miss nearly the entire season. Anderson was having continuing problems with his shins and had undergone surgery to see if they could be stabilized.

New faces coming in included veteran forwards Dale Ellis and J. R. Reid, as well as guards Vinny Del Negro, Avery Johnson, and Lloyd Daniels. What seemed to be lacking was heavy duty help for David under the boards, as well as consistent scoring from the backcourt. The 1992-93 Spurs didn't seemed to be a really balanced or really deep team.

David and all the other NBA centers also had to face a new challenge that year. His name was Shaquille O'Neal, and he stood 7'1" and weighed 303 pounds. O'Neal had come out of Louisiana State University after his junior season and was considered the most imposing physical presence since Wilt Chamberlain. He had excellent skills, as well, and was expected to take his place alongside the trio of Ewing, Olajuwon, and Robinson. In addition, O'Neal had a charming, outgoing personality and quick smile. He would become the new center of attention in more ways than one.

It was apparent right from the start of the season that the Spurs were uncomfortable. Maybe it was the new players coming in, maybe it was adjusting to the coach. The team lost four of its first five games and looked out of sync. They would start to bounce back before the month ended behind some stellar play by David.

His biggest game came against the Seattle Supersonics. In that match he scored 42 points and added ten rebounds as the Spurs won, 104-97. David was Player of the Week in late November and the Spurs ended the month with a 5-6 record. Then during the first couple of weeks in December the team floundered again. They were looking like a .500 team that just wasn't putting it together.

Finally, it was determined that a change had to be made. Jerry Tarkanian didn't appear comfortable behind the bench and on December 18 he was relieved of his coaching duties. Bob Bass coached the game against the Mavericks that night and the Spurs won it, 122-101, as Sean Elliott had a career-high 41 points. After the game, the Spurs held a press conference to announce their new coach. Again, the team took the basketball world by surprise.

The new coach was John Lucas, a former star point guard who had played with several NBA teams. Lucas' coaching experience consisted of just a single season in the United States Basketball League, so his qualifications seemed questionable. But his USBL team, the Florida Tropics, was a very special kind of ball club. Many of its players were recovering addicts being given an opportunity to resurrect their professional careers. Lucas not only coached the team, but owned it as well.

The reason for Lucas' interest was well known. He was also a recovering addict and was heavily involved in helping drug and alcohol dependent people. The Houston-based John Lucas Enterprises consists of a number of drug-treatment programs and other endeavors to help athletes and others maintain their sobriety and work to improve the quality of their life.

With Lucas involved in so many drug-related programs and other enterprises, people wondered how he would have time to coach an NBA team. But the new coach came in with a world of enthusiasm, and his emotional intensity seemed to be catching. Lucas took over a lethargic, 9-11, team and coached it to four wins in five games before December was over.

One of the first players to make the new coach feel comfortable with the team was David. Lucas still attended Alcoholics Anonymous meetings and told the team he would be going to a meeting one afternoon before the team played that night. The coach was sitting at the AA session for a few minutes when the door opened and a very tall young man walked in. It was David.

"David doesn't even drink," Lucas said. "But he has a curious mind, and he's a supportive person. I knew that's why he was there, to find out what AA was about and to show me his support. That's what makes him such a great leader."

The team and new coach really meshed in January. Suddenly the Spurs were the hottest club in the league. David had something to celebrate that month. On January 3, Valerie Robinson gave birth to a baby boy, named David Maurice Robinson, Jr. On January 16, David took to the court against the Charlotte Hornets and scored a career-high 52 points.

For the month of January the Spurs were 12-2, bringing their overall record to 26-14. They once again seemed close to being one of the top teams in the league. David averaged 24.4 points, 12.9 rebounds, and 4.36 blocks for the month. Despite the rookie success of Shaquille O'Neal and the continued strong play of Ewing and Olajuwon, David still seemed to possess the most all-around skills, especially on those nights when he had it all going for him.

The club was 9-4 in February, giving them a 26-7 record under Lucas. The final game, on February 28, was with Shaquille O'Neal and Orlando before a national television audience. San Antonio won a hard-fought game, with David scoring 23 points, grabbing 16 rebounds, getting seven assists, four steals, and three blocks. It was one of those nights when he had it all going. And he easily outplayed O'Neal.

After that, the team's pace slowed. Sean Elliott, who was having his best season, missed four games with a bad back. David was slowed somewhat by a sore thumb and sore knee. The team was 8-8 in March and then just 6-7 in April. Once again they were looking like a .500 team as the Houston Rockets came on to take the division crown.

The Spurs finished the season at 49-33, six games behind Houston and two ahead of Utah. David wound up averaging 23.2 points for the year, ninth in the league and the same as the rookie O'Neal. Olajuwon scored at a 26.1 clip and Ewing at 24.2. All four were close.

David did drop off somewhat in rebounding. He had an 11.7 mark, also ninth. O'Neal was second at 13.9 behind leader Dennis Rodman of Detroit.

Olajuwon was fourth and Ewing seventh. David's 3.22 blocks placed him fifth, behind Olajuwon and O'Neal, and two other young centers, Dikembe Mutombo and Alonzo Mourning. So the competition was getting stronger. All told, it was not one of David's best seasons.

This time around he made just the All-NBA third team, and was on the All-Defensive second team. He was still up there, but what would make it all right was an NBA title, or, if not that, at least a very strong showing for the team in the playoffs.

It wouldn't be easy. In the first round the Spurs had to go up against the Portland Trailblazers, who were 51-31 in the regular season. With the opener at Portland, the Blazers looked to go one up. In a five-game series, the first game is very important. It was a close game and the Spurs finally gave an indication that they were ready for a strong playoff run. A pair of Sean Elliott free throws in the final five seconds gave them a clutch 87-86 victory.

Though the Blazers won Game 2, the Spurs returned to San Antonio in good shape. Rallying behind David's 26 points and 19 from Willie Anderson, the Spurs won, 107-101. Then in the fourth game they closed the Blazers out, winning in overtime, 100-97. David had his first playoff triple-double, scoring 20 points, grabbing 17 rebounds, and dishing off 11 assists.

The victory put the Spurs into the conference semifinals against the Phoenix Suns. This would be the big test. The Suns had an NBA best 62-20 record and were considered by many the strongest team in the league. The Suns had Charles Barkley, who would be named the NBA's Most Valuable Player, Kevin Johnson, Dan Majerle, and other fine players. When they won the first two games, 98-89 and 109-103, the Spurs looked done.

David had 32 and 27 points in the first two games, but he would have gladly traded them for a victory. Back in San Antonio, the Spurs got the balanced attack they needed. Carr had 21 points, Ellis 20, while Avery Johnson had 12 points, 15 assists, and 8 rebounds. The Spurs won, 111-96. The team had a much better chance of winning when David didn't have to carry so much of a load.

The Spurs won the next game because of David. He had a playoff career-high of 36 points, 21 in the second half, as the Spurs won easily, 117-103. Unfortunately the club lost rugged Antoine Carr to a sprained ankle. He would be lost for the rest of the playoffs.

Back in Phoenix for Game 5, the series took its final turn. The Suns won, 109-97, as Barkley scored 38. David and Dale Ellis had 24 each for the Spurs. In Game 6 the Spurs looked like they would pull even as they held a 10-point lead in the fourth period. Then the Suns rallied to produce a furious finish.

After David had hit two free throws to tie the game with seconds left, Barkley came back to hit a clutch jumper, putting the Suns in front, 102-100, with 1.8 seconds left. The Spurs inbounded to David, who tried a quick 20-footer to tie it. The ball skittered off the rim at the buzzer. The Suns had won and the Spurs were disappointed once again.

David's playoff stats were remarkably consistent with his regular season totals. In ten games he averaged 23.1 points, 12.6 rebounds, and 3.6 blocks. The bottom line, though, was that the Spurs were eliminated once more. David had been the prime mover in making the Spurs a playoff team in each of his four years in the league. Yet the team had never made a serious run at the title. There had already been some whispers among fans, writers, and even a few players.

Maybe David Robinson wasn't the player he was made out to be after all.

Chapter 10
Scoring Champ

It's hard to say whether David had become somewhat complacent in his approach to the game. His numbers were remarkably similar each year and his team had a winning record. Yet even with a changing supporting cast and several coaches, David and the Spurs had not made it past the second round of the playoffs. Though neither Ewing nor Olajuwon had yet led his team to a championship, both had reputations as warriors, players who went all out nearly all the time.

The David Robinson who would be starting his fifth NBA season in the fall of 1993 wasn't perceived that way. One newspaper story described the feeling about David as a "subtle but undeniable decline in his status around the league."

It said that his talent had never been questioned, but there was a feeling that "he was too much of a finesse player, too reliant on jump shots instead of inside power moves. In short, the thinking was that he was too soft to lead the Spurs to an NBA championship."

Perhaps the feeling came about because of the young centers in the league. O'Neal personified power. Shaq dunked with such authority that he had already destroyed two backboards. *Shaq Attaq* was already an NBA and commercial byword. Young Alonzo Mourning of the Charlotte Hornets was another very aggressive, almost hostile player who fought and scrapped for every inch on the court.

While David more than held his own with the youngsters, as well as with Ewing and Olajuwon, he seemed to be the only one of the top centers whose luster had been tarnished. Isiah Thomas, the great point guard of the Detroit Pistons and a two-time NBA champion, also made note of the situation. Thomas put it this way.

"David Robinson has always been nice and their team has always been nice. But do you want a bunch of guys who are nice all the time, or do you want to win championships?"

Again the implication was there. Both David and the Spurs had to toughen up. Perhaps the Spurs' management was thinking the same thing. On October 1, just about the time training camp began, the team made an almost shocking major trade. They sent Sean Elliott, who was coming off perhaps his finest season, and reserve David Wood to the Detroit Pistons. In return they received a reserve forward named Isiah Morris and the main man they were after—veteran forward Dennis Rodman.

Dennis Rodman! The guy with the nickname, "Worm!" Dennis Rodman, one of the most unpredictable players in the league, a guy considered a super flake by even his friends. Yes, that was the Dennis Rodman they wanted. And with good reason. The 6'8", 32-year-old forward was flat-out the best rebounder in the NBA. His rebounding stats over the past several seasons were throwback numbers to the days of Bill Russell and Wilt Chamberlain.

Rodman was a wild story just by himself. He didn't play basketball in high school, didn't even think about wanting to play until the age of 20. He was working as a janitor on the night shift at DFW Airport in Dallas, Texas, when he quit his job and enrolled at Cooke County Junior College in Gainesville, Texas. A year later he went to Southeastern Oklahoma State and became a three-time NAIA (National Association of Intercollegiate Athletes) All-American who averaged 24.4 points and 17.8 rebounds his senior year.

A 25-year-old rookie with the Pistons in 1986, Rodman became a fixture in Detroit and was a big part of the Pistons 1989 and 1990 title teams. Never a big scorer in the NBA, Rodman concentrated on defense and rebounding with incredible success.

He was Defensive Player of the Year in both 1990 and 1991 as his rebound totals rose each season. By 1991 he had 1,026 boards for an average of 12.5 a game. But the next year, 1991-92, Rodman seemed to have made a decision to become an even better rebounder. At 6'8" he simply began outhustling and out-scrapping bigger and stronger men for the basketball.

When the season ended, he had 1,530 rebounds, an average of 18.7 a game. Needless to say, he led the league. In fact, it was the highest rebounding average since 1971-72, when Chamberlain averaged 19.2 boards a game. Rodman's work ethic was admired around the league. But he also had an unpredictable personality and sometimes explosive temper. He marched to his own drummer and was difficult to discipline.

Yet he continued to rebound like no one else. Though limited to 62 games because of injury and suspension in 1992-93, he still averaged 18.3 boards a game and made the NBA All-Defensive first team for the fifth straight season.

There were still questions. How would Rodman react in a new environment? Could John Lucas control and discipline him? At nearly 33 years of age would he be in decline? And most important of all, how would the undisciplined, unpredictable Rodman get along with the disciplined, conservative team leader, David Robinson. It was a mix the entire league would be watching.

As strange as he sometimes behaved, Rodman had a work ethic that David and the other Spurs admired. He worked out both before and after games on a stairmaster, treadmill, or exercise bike. On the court he was perpetual motion. And when the ball was up for grabs, Rodman would go up three and four times, tipping it, fighting for it, and not quitting until he got it.

Isiah Thomas, who said that David and the Spurs were too nice, also felt his former teammate would make a huge difference to his new team, and especially to its star center. "If Dennis can keep David angry, the Spurs could make it out of the West," Thomas said.

When Rodman arrived in camp he told Coach Lucas that he hoped there wasn't a team dress code because he wasn't big on suits and ties. Lucas smiled and said, "Just keep your shoelaces tied."

That was the way to handle Rodman. Give him room to be Rodman. During the season it became a guessing game what color his hair would be. It was blond much of the time, but he also showed up with it red, blue, and purple on occasion. He would miss meetings and some practices. But on the court he immediately resumed his position as the top rebounder in the league and the Spurs began winning.

The team was playing with a new kind of verve and fire. David didn't go around with a scowl on his face, like Ewing and Mourning, but he was playing with more ferocity. And, lo and behold, he and Rodman became fast friends, although an odd couple of sorts. Their friendship was based on mutual respect for each other's talents.

"Dennis brings a different kind of fire to the game, a fire you can't help but feel," David said. "I was too much of a gentleman; he was too wild. But he's made the game fun again for me.

"The best way I can describe it is that I don't feel like I'm going into battle unarmed anymore."

The Spurs got off to a fast start. They had a new home arena, the state-of-the-art Alamodome. That helped, too. But the Houston Rockets got off to an even faster start, winning their first 15 games of the season. San Antonio ended up chasing the Rockets nearly all season long. It was also the year of the big man. Suddenly all eyes were on Olajuwon, Robinson, Ewing, and O'Neal. For a good part of the season they were the top four scorers in the league. All four were playing for winning teams and racking up the numbers.

Before the season was even two months old there was talk about the change in David. He was going to the hoop more, concentrating harder on offense, and showing a new kind of desire to get things done. There was talk, even early in the year, of David being a genuine MVP candidate. One of his biggest boosters was newcomer Rodman.

"David's got so much talent it's ridiculous," Rodman said, then adding in characteristic fashion, "It's a pleasure to go out and play basketball with him."

Though David's game was more intense, he still maintained the same calm demeanor. As teammate Dale Ellis put it, "I'm still waiting for the first time I see David Robinson angry."

David didn't have to show his anger on the court. He was showing it with his numbers. At one point in midseason, the Spurs went on a tear that saw them win 25 of 30 games. David had a 50-point game against the Timberwolves and a 46-point effort against the Celtics. He seemed to be winning

Player of the Week honors with regularity. He would take that honor five times during the season.

In the 50-point outing against the Timberwolves it was Coach Lucas who sent David back into the game late in the fourth quarter specifically to reach that 50-point plateau.

"He looked at me like I was crazy when I told him I wanted him to go back in," Lucas said. "But I want David to be a little greedy, because that can make us better. I want to have to hold up the team bus because he can't get through all the people who want his autograph—because the bigger he gets, the better we get."

David was still the key, the main man. Even Rodman knew it. "The Spurs have always been a team that got their 50, 55 wins and didn't do much of anything in May and June," Rodman said. "We're fixin' to change that. I can clear us a little path, but David's the one who's got to lead the way."

David still wasn't a traditional post-up center. Both Olajuwon and O'Neal would post up close in, back to the basket. The offense would then revolve around them, with the guards trying to get the ball into the post and run plays off that. Olajuwon had a variety of spin and fade moves. He could get the fadeaway jumper or drive right to the hoop. He could also turn and take a traditional jump shot. He had an extremely quick first step and was hard to stop.

O'Neal also played close in. Being just a second year player, he was still developing moves and shots. In close, however, he was always a threat to jam, and with 300 pounds of muscle, not too many defenders got in his way. Ewing played it both ways. He sometimes set up back to the basket. But his favorite shot was the jumper, and he was often criticized for not going to the hoop enough.

David also liked to play facing the basket where he could see more of the court. The offense was set up so that he would be facing the hoop more of the time. His jump shot had become more reliable, to the point where he would also shoot longer three-point shots more than ever before. His quickness enabled him to get to the hoop, take an offensive rebound, and slam the ball, or be the trailer on a drive. And he still ran the floor better than any other big man in the game.

On the night of February 17, David and his teammates took the court against the Detroit Pistons. It was a night David had it going on all burners. He did all the things he was supposed to do and more. When the game ended, San Antonio had an easy victory and David had just achieved the fourth quadruple-double in NBA history. That means being in double figures in four different categories. For the game David had 34 points, 12 rebounds, ten assists, and ten blocked shots.

In fact, he would record five triple-doubles during the season (including the quadruple), the most in the league. The only stat that was down somewhat was his rebounds. He was still averaging over ten a game, but he had the luxury of letting that slide a bit. That's because Rodman was grabbing more than 17 a game, and once again leading the league by a wide margin.

As the season began winding down, the Spurs were battling the Rockets for the division lead, and David was locked in a battle with Shaq for the scoring crown. Olajuwon was also having a brilliant season, and most observers figured the MVP would be David or Olajuwon. One player who thought the Admiral was the man was John Salley of the Miami Heat, who was also a former teammate of Rodman's with Detroit.

"The Spurs are playing great and David's the MVP right now," Salley said. "If he keeps playing the way he's playing, they'll be tough all the way through the playoffs. Dennis will show him the road to victory."

Even David gave Rodman credit for the change in the team and in his own game. The taller member of basketball's odd couple put it this way.

"I've been around Michael Jordan and Charles Barkley and Larry Bird," David said, "but I've learned more about winning from Dennis Rodman than from any player I've ever come in contact with."

In the final week of the season it looked as if the Rockets would take the division with the Spurs right behind. The scoring title was still up for grabs, with O'Neal holding a paper-thin lead over David, and Olajuwon third. Because of his stellar all-around play, Olajuwon was now just slightly ahead of David in the minds of most as far as the league MVP was concerned.

It came down to the final game of the year. The Rockets had already wrapped up the Midwest

Division, and as the Spurs took to the court against the L.A. Clippers, only the scoring title was at stake. O'Neal had a very slim lead and would be finishing his season against the New Jersey Nets.

David began scoring early and his teammates began feeding him the ball. It was apparent that they wanted him to get that scoring crown. The game was close as well. The Clippers wanted to finish on a high note and began double- and triple-teaming David, often fouling him when he got the ball and began to make his move. He was hitting his free throws, then coming downcourt and doing it again.

"It was unbelievable," David said. "My team has been behind me the whole year. They always push me to do a lot of individual things. As a leader, I just try to win games, but tonight they really wanted me to shoot it. When the game started they were looking for me almost every time."

In the second half, David went over the 50-point mark and kept shooting. Then he topped the 60-point mark. It wasn't until late in the game that the Spurs began to pull away, so David had to keep shooting for the victory as well. When the final buzzer sounded, San Antonio had a 112-97 win and David Robinson had a total of—71 points!

It was an amazing finish. David had hit on 26 of 41 shots from the floor and 18 of 25 from the free throw line. He was only the fourth player in NBA history to score more than 70 points in a game. The others were Wilt Chamberlain, David Thompson, and Elgin Baylor. When it was over, even David couldn't believe it.

"I looked up at the scoreboard," he exclaimed, "and I said, '71 points, oh, my goodness!'"

Shaquille O'Neal had a normally outstanding game in his finale. He scored 32. When the final tallies were made, David had won the scoring championship, averaging 29.79 points in 80 games. Shaq averaged 29.35 points in 81 games for the Orlando Magic. In total points, they were just six points apart, 2,383 to 2,377.

As for the team, the Spurs were at 55-27 for the year, three games behind Houston in the Midwest, placing them at that 55-win level again. Now they had to deal with the playoffs. Otherwise, David and his teammates would not look at it as a successful season.

It certainly had been successful in other ways. Rodman led the league in rebounding with a 17.3 average, while David averaged 10.7 a game. David was also third behind Mutombo and Olajuwon in blocked shots with 3.31 a game. Amazingly enough, he also led the Spurs in assists with a career-best 381, an average of 4.8 per game. That was also the most assists of any frontcourt player in the league. In addition, David was the first center to lead the league in scoring since Bob McAdoo in 1975-76. He also played the most minutes of his career, 3,241, for an average of 40.5 a game.

"David went above and beyond the call of duty this year," said a Spurs teammate. "He may have been inspired by Dennis, but he also pushed to go that extra mile for all of us."

In the first round of the playoffs the Spurs

would meet the Utah Jazz, a team that finished just two games behind them in the division. The Jazz had superstars Karl Malone and John Stockton and matched up very well with the Spurs. It wouldn't be an easy series.

It opened at the Alamodome and in the first game the Spurs looked like they meant business. The team launched a balanced attack and burst into a 55-43 halftime lead, opening it up to 82-61 after three quarters. From there they cruised to a 106-89 victory. David had 25 points. Terry Cummings, who had recovered from his knee injury to play eight games at the end of the year, came through with 18 points. Anderson had 15 and Del Negro 12, while Rodman had 11 rebounds. It was the kind of team play the ball club needed to win.

But in Game 2, also at the Alamodome, things began to go sour. The Spurs took a 24-20 lead after one quarter, then suddenly began to play as if there were a lid on the basket. At one point in the second and third quarters, the team missed 25 straight shots. They scored just nine in the second period and 16 in the third, shooting just five for 34 during that span. By the end of the third quarter they were trailing 75-49 and completely demoralized.

The final was 96-84. David had just 12 points and hit just two of 14 from the field. It was a fiasco.

"Nothing went right; nothing went in, and that's the end of it," David said. "We have to forget it and go on from here."

The problem was they also had to go to Utah, where the Jazz always played very well. Nor did it help that the Spurs wouldn't have Rodman available. He was suspended for Game 3 after an altercation in the second game. That made it easier for the Jazz, who won the game by the embarrassing score of 105-72. The Spurs seemed to be falling apart at the seams.

They made the fourth game closer, but by then it was too late. Utah won, 95-90, to eliminate the Spurs in the first round once more. David scored 27 with 12 rebounds. Ellis had 24 and Rodman returned to grab 20 rebounds. It wasn't enough. Karl Malone and company closed them out.

It was a very bitter ending to what had been a banner season in so many ways. A short time later, David learned that Hakeem Olajuwon had been named the league's Most Valuable Player. Olajuwon got 66 first place votes for 889 points, while David finished second with 24 first place votes and 730 points. Scottie Pippen of the Bulls was a distant third.

It would be Olajuwon's year. He was also named Defensive Player of the Year and would lead his team to the NBA title, beating Ewing and the Knicks in the Finals. There could be no complaints about his selection.

David did win one postseason prize. He was given the NBA's IBM Award, which was based on a computerized rating that determines a player's overall contribution to his team's success. David was also on the All-Defensive second team. There is no doubt that he continues to be one of the best.

In many ways, David Robinson is a happy man.

He still has his varied interests. He usually travels with a keyboard and also plays his saxophone as much as possible. In fact, he once played sax with jazz star Branford Marsalis. He is a frequent guest on television talk shows and continues to do his charity work, much of it with the David Robinson Foundation. He also plays golf, and says his perfect vacation is "relaxing at home with my wife and our son."

Despite all his basketball success at Navy and then in the NBA, David still hasn't experienced the sweet taste of victory that comes only with an NBA championship. He saw in 1994 what winning did for Hakeem Olajuwon. Always a great player, Olajuwon was universally recognized in 1994 as one of those players with the talent and leadership to take his team to the very top.

The Spurs will once again do some retooling. After the 1993-94 season, they released Operations Director Bob Bass, then saw John Lucas resign and move over to the Philadelphia 76ers. The team hired a new coach in 1994-95, Bob Hill.

David has always been able to adjust to coaching changes and new teammates while continuing to play well. But he won't be completely satisfied until he and his teammates can sit in the winner's circle and bask in the glory of an NBA title. For a basketball player like David Robinson, that is the ultimate goal, the only goal. Nothing's better.

David Robinson Statistics

United States Naval Academy

Year	G	FGM-A	Pct.	FTM-A	Pct.	Reb.	A	Blk	Pts.	Avg.
83-84	28	86-138	.623	42-73	.575	111	6	37	214	7.6
84-85	32	302-469	.626	152-243	.626	370	19	128	756	23.6
85-86	35	294-484	.607	208-331	.628	455	24	207	796	22.7
86-87	32	350-592	.591	202-317	.637	378	33	144	903	28.2
Total	127	1032-1683	.613	604-964	.627	1314	82	516	2669	21.0

San Antonio Spurs

Year	G	FGM-A	Pct.	FTM-A	Pct.	Reb.	A	Blk	Pts.	Avg.
89-90	82	690-1300	.531	613-837	.732	983	164	319	1993	24.3
90-91	82	754-1366	.552	592-777	.762	1063	208	320	2101	25.6
91-92	68	592-1074	.551	393-561	.701	829	181	305	1578	23.2
92-93	82	676-1348	.501	561-766	.732	956	301	264	1916	23.4
93-94	80	840-1658	.507	693-925	.749	855	381	265	2383	29.8
Total	394	3552-6746	.527	2852-3866	.738	4686	1235	1473	9971	25.3

Honors

United States Naval Academy

1985-86

First & Second Team All-American

Led Nation in Rebounding

Led Nation in Blocked Shots

1986-87

Consensus First Team All-American

College Basketball Player of the Year

Led Nation in Blocked Shots

San Antonio Spurs

1989-90

NBA Rookie of the Year

Schick Award Winner

All-Rookie First Team

All-NBA Third Team

All-Defensive Second Team

1990-91

All-NBA First Team

NBA Rebounding Champion

Schick Award Winner

All-Defensive First Team

1991-92

NBA Defensive Player of the Year
All-NBA First Team
NBA Blocked Shots Champion
All-Defensive First Team

1992-93

All-NBA Third Team
All-Defensive Second Team

1993-94

NBA Scoring Champion
All-NBA Second Team
All-Defensive Second Team

If you like **A TO Z MYSTERIES**®, take a swing at

BALLPARK® *Mysteries*

#1: The Fenway Foul-Up

#2: The Pinstripe Ghost

#3: The L.A. Dodger

#4: The Astro Outlaw

#5: The All-Star Joker

#6: The Wrigley Riddle

#7: The San Francisco Splash

#8: The Missing Marlin

#9: The Philly Fake

#10: The Rookie Blue Jay

#11: The Tiger Troubles

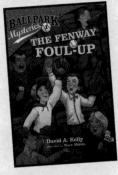